Supervisor's Guide To Contract Administration and Grievance Handling

by
Joseph J. Woodford

This book presents authoritative information on contract administration and grievance handling. There are many factors that affect the interpretation and application of a specific collective bargaining agreement. Therefore, supervisors are encouraged to seek legal advice or other expert assistance regarding specific questions about grievances or the interpretation and application of their collective bargaining agreements.

Special thanks to the following who gave of their time to read and criticize the text:

Douglas A. Brown, Ph.D
Executive Director, School Employers Association

A. L. Bruton
Assistant to Superintendent, San Bernardino City Schools

Edward J. Kelly
Chief of Employee Relations, County of San Bernardino

Ronald C. Ruud
Attorney, Atkinson, Andelson, Loya, Ruud and Romo

First Printing, June 1986
Second Printing, May 1990
Third Printing, October 1996

Printed in the United States of America

Library of Congress Catalog Card Number: 86-70053
ISBN 0-913409-05-7

ADVISORY PUBLISHING & CONSULTING
P.O. Drawer 3277 Crestline, CA 92325
(909) 338-5103

ABOUT THE AUTHOR

Joseph J. Woodford is a graduate of California State University Long Beach. While employed by the City of Gardena from 1969 to 1972, he completed his post-graduate work at Long Beach. He was that City's chief spokesman in negotiations with three employee organizations in addition to taking charge of most other personnel functions. From municipal management he moved to a position with organized labor. As Chief of Representation for the Service Employees International Union, AFL-CIO, Local 960, he supervised a professional staff engaged in providing complete representation services to over sixty bargaining units. From 1972 through 1977, he personally negotiated over 100 collective bargaining agreements in addition to other experiences in unit determinations, representation elections, disciplinary appeals, and arbritations. He is currently Director of Employee Relations for the San Bernardino City Unified School District where he is the Board's Chief Negotiator in collective bargaining with three units covering about 5,000 employees. Over the past nine years, he has been active as a speaker, trainer and instructor in the field of labor relations and employee discipline. Joe is the co-author of the very popular *Supervisor's Guide to Documentation and File Building for Employee Discipline.* In addition, he is associate editor of the Association of California School Administrators' "Strike Manual." In October, 1985, Joe was honored by his peers when he received the Association of California School Administrators "Negotiator of the Year" award.

CONTENTS

PREFACE

In the early 1970's a good friend, Robert Austin, and I developed and began conducting a number of workshops for both labor and management in applied labor relations. Those workshops were presented through a grant from the United States Civil Service Commission under the Intergovernmental Personnel Act. The contents of these workshops were based on our interest in labor relations and on our practical experience as both labor and management advocates. The workshops were designed to show supervisors and union stewards how to handle day-to-day labor relations problems. "Contract Administration and Grievance Handling" is one workshop that evolved from those early efforts.

Over the years I have accumulated new information on the subject and have revised the workshop regularly. This book represents that workshop as it has evolved over the past 15 years with new materials presented in the book that could not be presented in a one-day training program.

Some of the ideas used in my workshop and in this book were adapted from "Collective Bargaining for Public Managers" produced by the United States Civil Service Commission, Bureau of Training, Labor Relations Training Center. Other materials have been gathered from a variety of sources. Unfortunately, the identity of many of these sources has been lost through revisions of the original material.

Grateful acknowledgement is made to the California League of City Employee Associations and the San Bernardino City Unified School District, as it was while in their employ that I was allowed to experiment in labor relations training. Recognition must be given to the following organizations whose meetings, seminars and published literature have supplied the basis for some of the ideas and concepts used:

American Arbitration Association
Association of California School Administrators
Inland Personnel Council

National Public Employers Labor Relations Association
School Employers Association
Service Employees International Union
UCLA Institute of Industrial Relations
United States Department of Labor

Special thanks and recognition is given to my wife, Patti, for typing and retyping the manuscript so many times on her computer.

INTRODUCTION

When a union organizes a group of employees and negotiates a contract, many of the old ways of dealing with employees by supervisors must give way. The contract takes away the ability of the supervisor to make decisions based upon his own subjective determinations. The work place is now governed by a legally enforceable collective bargaining agreement that limits the rights of management.

Supervisors must learn new rules and techniques for dealing with employees and their union. Failure to learn these new rules often results in a loss of important remaining management rights, unnecessary conflict between labor and management and decreased productivity. Because of these costly consequences, no employer with organized employees can afford to let supervisors administer the contract and handle grievances by the old trial and error method.

Contract administration and grievance handling are important management functions. The action or inaction of supervisors will determine the success or failure of the employer's labor relations program. Unfortunately, few employers in industry and government systematically train supervisors in the skills required to administer the collective bargaining agreement and to handle employee grievances.

Supervisors need both training and experience to acquire real expertise in contract administration and in handling grievances. Since ineffective contract management and grievance processing often result in erosion or surrender of management rights and poor labor relations, it is vital that supervisors know how to interpret and apply the contract and to properly respond to a grievance.

Unions know that they can make significant improvements in working conditions during the life of the collective bargaining agreement. The practices, precedents and grievance settlements created under the contract often become binding as if they were written into the contract. This phenomenon gives rise to the old union saying, "What we don't get at the bargaining table, we'll get through grievances." Unfortunately, this becomes a reality for many employers. Management negotiates with unions and refuses to give in on a particular working condition only to find that untrained supervisors have given it away at the work place.

The better unions spend considerable time and effort training stewards. The untrained supervisor is often no match for the steward who has completed many hours of training on the details of the contract and how to process grievances. A cadre of well-trained stewards facing untrained supervisors will strip away management's rights to run the enterprise.

The purpose of this book is to provide supervisors and managers with proven methods to successfully administer collective bargaining agreements and process grievances. The principles and techniques are simple and straightforward, yet few supervisors and managers in either government or business have gained a high level of competency. By applying a few basic principles, the supervisor will command the necessary skills to:

1. Preserve management's rights;
2. Deal effectively with union representation;
3. Prevent grievances;
4. Manage the grievance procedure;
5. Conduct grievance meetings;
6. Answer grievances;
7. Resolve conflicts;
8. Interpret contract language;
9. Discipline employees for just cause; and
10. Testify at arbitration hearings.

With these skills supervisors will have the confidence to meet any challenge presented by a unionized work force.

This book is designed to show the supervisor, in simple terms and by use of examples, check lists, and other aids, "how to" administer union contracts and handle grievances. It is intended to be a ready desk-reference and practical guide to be used on a day-to-day basis in the work place. The author hopes this effort will in some way contribute to the efficiency of government and business by assisting management in preserving its right to run the enterprise.

CHAPTER ONE

The Collective Bargaining Process

The history of organized labor in the United States begins in 1778 when journeymen printers in New York City combined to demand an increase in wages. After the increase was granted, the organization was abandoned. In 1926 the first federal collective bargaining statute, the Railway Labor Act, became law. It required employers to bargain collectively and not discriminate against their employees for joining a union. In 1935 the National Labor Relations (Wagner) Act established the first national labor policy of protecting the right of workers to organize and to elect their representatives for collective bargaining. The Labor Management Relations (Taft-Hartley) Act became law in 1947 creating a new national labor policy. Over the years the Labor Management Relations Act has been amended a number of times.

The Labor Management Relations Act covers employers and employees in the private sector, but not all private sector employers are included. Most states have enacted collective bargaining rights for state and local government employees. The federal government has granted its employees collective bargaining rights by executive order. All collective bargaining laws provide a systematic procedure for resolution of conflict in the work place.

Collective bargaining can best be understood by viewing the law as a series of stages. The first stage is the unorganized stage. During this stage there is no union representing or attempting to represent the employees in collective bargaining. The employer is free to unilaterally establish personnel policies defining terms and conditions of employment. Individual employees may negotiate their own employment contracts.

When a union mounts a campaign among the employees to gain the right to become their exclusive representative in collective bargaining, the process enters the second stage. The organizing stage is characterized by union organizers and a committee of employees gathering employee signatures on authorization cards. During this stage the law drastically restricts what an employer may do in dealing with its employees. In general, all collective bargaining laws prohibit employers from restraining, coercing or interfering with employees in the exercise of their collective bargaining rights. No discrimination against employees because of their union activities or membership is lawful. Employers should provide supervisors with specific instructions governing their conduct during an organizing campaign.

Third is the petition stage. At this point the union either asks the employer to recognize it as representing company employees, or it asks the appropriate labor board, such as the National Labor Relations Board (NLRB), to conduct an election. The petition must be supported by a showing of interest among the employees. For example, the NLRB requires a 30 percent showing of interest in order to call an election.

The unit determination stage is fourth in the series. At this point a decision is made as to the appropriate unit — the group of employees designated for representation by an employee organization when it negotiates a collective bargaining agreement. This composition of the unit is often hotly contested between the union or unions and management. The final decision on unit determination is often made by the labor board. It could be, for example, an employer-wide unit, blue collar unit, departmental unit or craft unit.

After an appropriate unit is established, an election date is set as the process moves into stage five. Official notices are posted where employees normally gather. This stage is characterized by campaigning and propaganda. Some employers, especially in the private sector, will actively campaign to get the employees to vote against having any union representation. There are many specific rules governing the conduct of both labor and management during the election period.

Sixth is the certification and recognition stage. If a majority of the employees vote for a union, it is certified as the representative for purposes of collective bargaining. With certification and recognition, the union gains certain legal rights and obligations as the representative of employees in the unit. New legal obligations are imposed on the employer, including a requirement to meet and negotiate in good faith with the union.

Preparation for negotiations marks the seventh stage. Actually, this planning and preparation should begin when the union first appears on the scene, and resumes as soon as the first contract is signed. Thereafter there is no end to planning and preparation for contract negotiations. It is continuous in a process that lasts as long as the union is certified to represent employees in the unit.

Eighth is the negotiation stage. Few supervisors are directly involved in contract negotiations as members of management negotiating teams. There are, however, at least two important reasons why supervisors must understand contract negotiations. During negotiations the supervisor has a role in providing informational support to upper management. Supervisors who understand the dynamics and effects of contract negotiations are better able to administer the collective bargaining agreement. The supervisor is management's closest contact with the employee. The supervisor sometimes hears rumors concerning union proposals and demands, its bargaining plans and strategies and/or conflicts between union factions. Without prying into union business, the supervisor gains access to valuable information that can be useful to the employer's negotiators. Open channels of communications from middle to top management is a role for supervisors during the negotiations stage.

The ninth and final stage involves contract administration. After the contract is signed, it becomes legally binding and responsibility shifts to the supervisor to administer it on a day-to-day basis. The contract administration stage, like the preparation for negotiations stage, is continuous.

Since a contract is a product of compromise, there is no such thing as a perfect collective bargaining agreement. Even though imperfect, the contract defines wages, hours, benefits and various terms and conditions of employment in a way agreed upon by both labor and management. It is critical that supervisors not only know the contents of the contract, but also the employer's interpretation of each clause.

The supervisor is the vital link in the chain of command that converts the collective bargaining agreement into practice. During the contract administration stage the employer has an obligation and right to continue to run the enterprise through its designated managers and supervisors. The union, through its representatives, polices management's actions to insure compliance with the terms of the collective bargaining agreement. If the union thinks that management has violated the contract, it may challenge management's action by filing a grievance. Conflict is typically resolved through a negotiated grievance procedure.

The following chart shows the nine stages of the collective bargaining process. The preparation for negotiations and contract administration stages are both continuous. Supervisors have a major responsibility for contract administration.

THE COLLECTIVE BARGAINING PROCESS

- PROVIDES SYSTEMATIC PROCEDURES FOR RESOLUTION OF CONFLICT

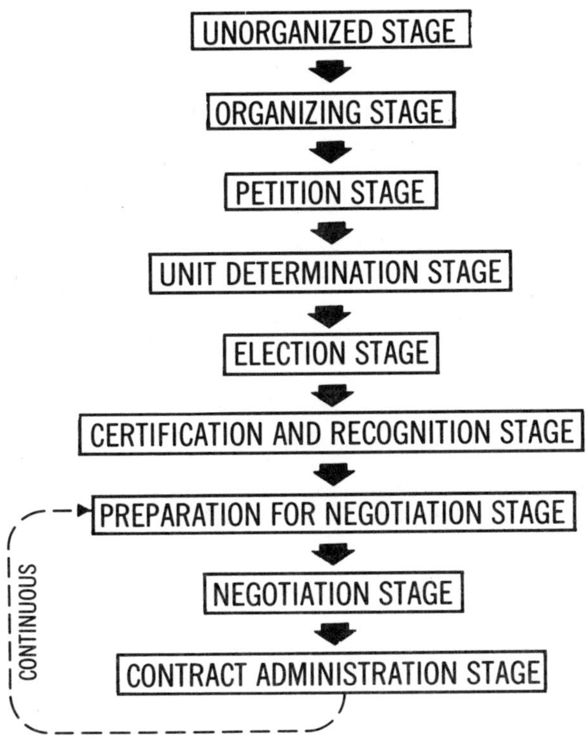

CHAPTER TWO

Contract Administration

Negotiations are over. Now the long period of administering the collective bargaining agreement begins. This is the stage of the collective bargaining process where labor and management spend most of their time.

But are negotiations really over? Frequently, it is simply that negotiations of a different sort are beginning. The union attempts to influence day-to-day decisions so as to gain advantages they could not achieve at the bargaining table. What was thought to be clear and unambiguous contract language now is found to have several possible meanings. The union will use its influence, and possibly the grievance procedure, to secure the interpretations that diminish management's rights.

No collective bargaining agreement is immune from interpretation problems. Even the best negotiators cannot think of every contingency that may occur in the work place. If the negotiators could anticipate all possible problems in interpretation, the need to compromise in order to reach an agreement precludes writing a perfect contract. Thus, the collective bargaining agreement is a dynamic document that is subject to gradual change as it is put into use through daily interpretations.

Effective contract administration depends on the supervisor. The daily decision making of supervisors throughout the organization will often determine the success or failure of the employer's labor relations program. All the time and money spent in preparation for collective bargaining, careful drafting of contract language and supervisory training may be rendered useless by poor administration of the contract by a supervisor.

During contract administration the agreement becomes more than words on paper. Actions by supervisors give the words meaning in the work place. To understand this, divide the contract administration stage into three functions:

1. INTERPRETATION of the contract language;
2. IMPLEMENTATION of the contract language; and
3. INCORPORATION of the precedents and practices established through implementation, into the contract.

Known as the three "I's" of contract administration, these functions are interrelated.

Supervisors interpret the contract and implement it based upon their interpretations. In other words, the supervisor directly applies contract provisions to specific work situations. If the union disagrees with the applications, it may challenge them through the grievance procedure. Or, the union may allow the incorporation of the practices through inaction.

Under the pressure of getting the job done, with deadlines, supervisors frequently cut corners. All too often this results in an erosion of management rights. Typically, management rights are diminished by supervisors who:

1. Do not know or understand the provisions of the collective bargaining agreement;
2. Fail to uniformly and consistently enforce all provisions of the contract;
3. Overlook continued minor violations of rules by employees;
4. Make verbal side agreements with employees or their union steward;
5. Approve or go along with some expeditious but incorrect contract interpretation; or
6. Grant grievances that should be denied.

Supervisors must avoid falling into the trap of taking the easy way out in contract administration. This approach incorporates into the agreement practices that weaken management rights.

Good contract administration results in the preservation of management rights. Knowledge is the first step towards successful contract administration. The supervisor must read the contract from cover to cover. Any areas the supervisor does not fully understand should be noted. He should review these questions with the employer's labor relations representative. It is important for the supervisor to know the intent of the clauses he must implement. Knowledge of the contract is necessary in order to interpret and implement the contract.

Also important for good contract administration is knowledge of what management's negotiators refused to include in the collective bargaining agreement. This information is an aid in determining the mutual intent of contract language. Management's negotiator is the best source of this information.

Some employers help supervisors administer the contract by preparing an annotated version of the contract. The annotated contract contains a provision-by-provision, written explanation of the background and intent of the contract. Almost all employers train supervisors through regular briefings following negotiations. In addition, supervisors should meet several times during the life of the contract to discuss problems and share experiences. This also helps to maintain consistency and uniformity throughout the organization.

Uniform and consistent interpretation and implementation of contract provisions is the goal of contract administration. Without uniform interpretation, supervisors may unknowingly give away in administration what the employer's negotiators refused to give up at the bargaining table. For example, if two supervisors apply a contract provision differently, the steward in the area where the provision is most narrowly interpreted will push his supervisor to adopt the more liberal interpretation of the other supervisor. This is called "whip-sawing."

The contract must be applied consistently to all employees in the bargaining unit. Unequal treatment will usually result in a grievance and another opportunity for the union to try and whip-saw management in order to gain something it could not get in negotiations. Inconsistent application of the contract only gives the union another shot at weakening management rights.

Supervisors must enforce the employer's work rules under the contract. Even though violations may be minor, the supervisor must take steps to get all employees to conform. Failure to enforce a rule or the lax enforcement of a rule may result in a new practice which, over time, may nullify the rule. In other words, supervisory inaction may incorporate new terms and conditions of employment into the contract.

It is dangerous for supervisors to make verbal side agreements that deviate from the contract with employees or the union representative. Supervisors cannot count on union leadership to remain stable. If the steward changes, the supervisor cannot be sure that the new steward will abide by a "gentleman's agreement." Even if the steward doesn't change, the steward may be forced by union politics to renege on the deal. The contract should only be changed through renegotiations and not through agreements on the shop floor.

Once a supervisor determines what his interpretation of a contract provision is and begins to apply it, he is incorporating a practice into the contract. Practices, although they may never be reduced to writing, become, over a period of time, as strong as a written clause in the contract. Management rights often suffer when supervisors fail to uniformly and consistently apply the contract, fail to enforce rules and make deals that don't conform to the contract. The supervisor's interpretations and implementation of the contract, whether by direct action or inaction, are incorporated into the contract. Management rights are best preserved by supervisors who closely follow the written language of the contract.

HOW TO USE THIS CHART

This chart shows the three functions of the "Contract Administration Stage" which is a continuous process. After a collective bargaining agreement is negotiated, supervisors and managers make interpretations in response to day-to-day problems. Interpretation of the contract language is the first function of contract administration.

After the contract language is interpreted, it must be applied to specific job situations. When this occurs, the contract language is implemented. Implementation of contract language is the second function of contract administration.

The implementation of contract language creates practices. Over time, practices are incorporated into the contract. The third function of contract administration is the incorporation of the precedents and practices created by the interpretation and implementation functions into the contract.

Supervisors and managers may want to view contract administration as four questions:

1. What is the interpretation?
2. How do we apply it?
3. What practices are created?
4. How is the contract modified?

Contract administration is a dynamic process that continuously modifies the contract to reflect the various interpretations and applications of contract language made to meet the changing needs of the work place.

CONTRACT ADMINISTRATION STAGE
A CONTINUOUS PROCESS

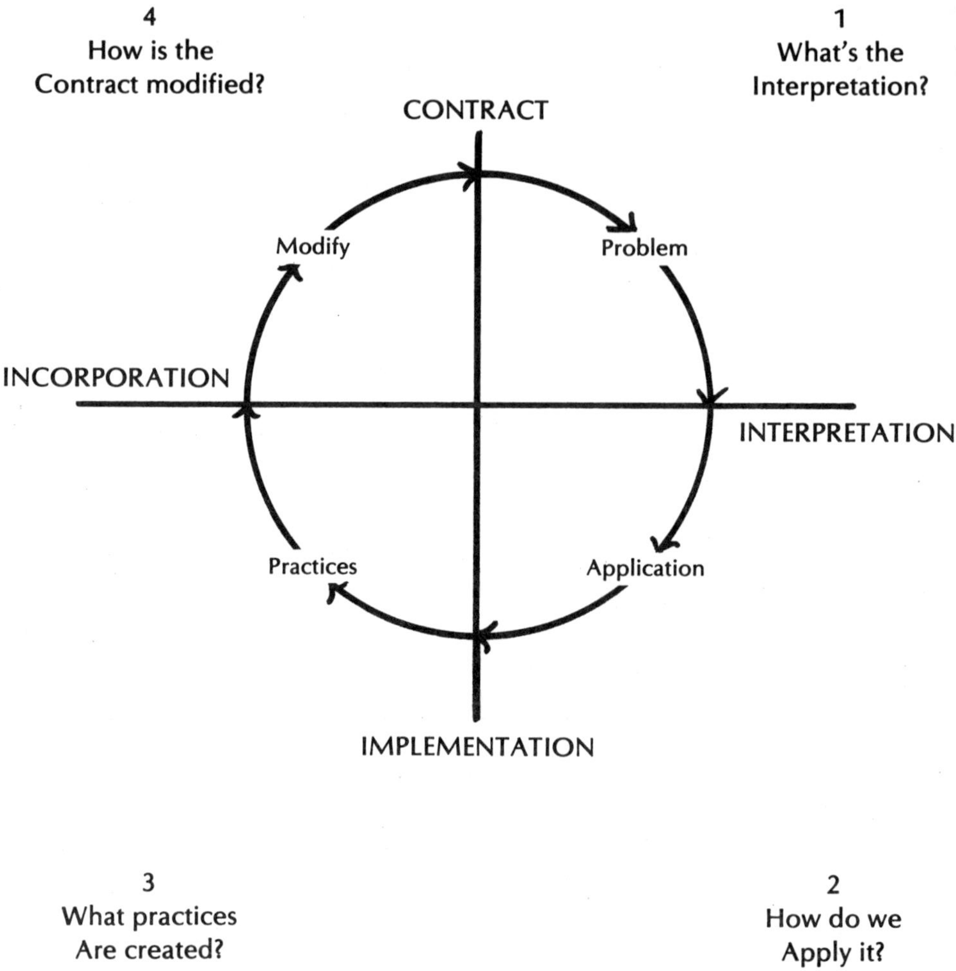

CHAPTER THREE

The Steward

The use of the term "steward" is not universal. It is, however, the most common name given to an employee who acts as a representative of other employees in a predefined work area. Whether called "steward," "shop steward," "job representative" or something else, this is the person whose job is to act as the primary link between the employees and their union and the supervisor.

The supervisor is the person most directly involved in contract administration. It is the supervisor who makes the collective bargaining agreement work. The union steward, by the same token, is the person who is most directly involved in policing the contract. It is vitally important that supervisors and managers understand the role the union steward plays in contract administration and grievance handling.

The union steward is an employee who has been selected to represent fellow workers. Some stewards are elected by the members. In other cases they are appointed by union officers or the union executive board. It is a good idea for the supervisor to know how the steward is selected. Knowledge of the method of selection will help the supervisor to understand the political pressures under which the steward operates.

In selecting a steward, union members look for the following qualifications and characteristics:

1. Active union member;
2. Strongly union oriented;

3. Intelligent;
4. Good communications skills;
5. Knowledgeable about the collective bargaining agreement; and
6. Willingness to serve as a steward.

Unfortunately, willingness to be a steward is often the most important consideration, especially when other union members are not interested in working as a steward.

Frequently, other factors may influence the selection of a steward. Some other common criteria in steward selection are:

1. Helped organize the union;
2. Member of union negotiating team;
3. Personal popularity among membership; and
4. Political payoff by the union.

Giving some thought to why a steward was chosen may help the supervisor to understand the steward's orientation.

Additional insight into the steward can be gained by asking, "Why does he want to be a steward?" Typical answers to this question are:

1. Seeks higher union office;
2. Looks for status and recognition;
3. Sees it as a road to promotion into supervision;
4. Likes to help people; or
5. Is a disgruntled troublemaker with an ax to grind against the employer.

It is important for supervisors to know the employee's motivation to become a steward. This will frequently help the supervisor to understand reasons for the steward's actions.

An effective steward fulfills many responsibilities. The steward has a role in contract administration to police the contract. The steward does not administer the contract —

that's the supervisor's job. By watching management's application of the contract at the work site, the steward is able to detect violations. Suspected violations of the agreement are then discussed with supervision. In this way the steward seeks to enforce the collective bargaining agreement.

The steward has a responsibility to assist employees in processing grievances. He will listen to employee gripes, complaints and problems. The steward will then follow up by investigating. This may include talking to other employees, reviewing records and discussions with the supervisor. If the steward thinks that the contract may have been violated, he will help the employee in filing a grievance. The steward may represent the aggrieved employee at meetings with supervision and other levels of management. The effective steward will make sure that the employee properly follows the negotiated grievance procedure so as to not forfeit any rights the employee has under the contract.

A union's strength is its membership. Since not all collective bargaining agreements require a union shop, the steward helps by recruiting new members. By performing this important responsibility, the steward insures the survival of the union as new people enter the bargaining unit. Failure to capture new members threatens the union's existence. Thus, effective stewards insure the existence of their union.

The steward acts as the union's eyes and ears at the work place. This communication link from the steward to higher union officials allows the union to monitor the employer's administration of the contract. The steward also serves as a communication link between the union and the membership. The steward provides regular communications to union members on a variety of matters; such as, union policy, status of negotiations, working conditions, union meetings, etc. The steward also serves as a communications link with management. The effective steward will keep supervision informed about the union's position on the application of the contract and will maintain a constructive relationship with the supervisor.

Ideally, stewards will be trained by their union to properly handle these responsibilities. Stewards should be trained to know their contract. In addition, stewards should receive training on employer policies and procedures that affect employees and important state and federal labor laws. In order to be effective representatives, stewards may receive specialized training in handling grievances. The good steward will know the grievance procedure forward and backward.This knowledge, combined with good listening and advocacy skills, will represent a challenge for even the best trained supervisor.

Most unions supplement steward training with a steward's manual. A synopsis of a steward's manual is included at the end of this CHAPTER. Training and a steward's manual do not guarantee that all stewards will be able to do the job. Just as there are good and bad supervisors, stewards are of varying quality.

Because of their jobs, there is bound to be conflict between the steward and the supervisor. One obvious area of conflict is when the steward polices the contract. The supervisor's interpretation will favor management by getting the job done, saving money or increasing productivity. The steward's interpretations will favor employees by minimizing their job obligations and giving maximum employee rights and job protection. Conflict may arise over other issues such as the use of employer time by the steward to transact union business and investigation of grievances. It is important that supervisors understand the responsibilities of the steward so that potential for conflict can be dealt with without hostility.

Hostility often arises because the steward must represent all unit members, right or wrong. This is analogous to a citizen's right to an attorney. An effective, well-trained steward will try to discourage grievances which he believes are unjustified. Such discouragement is not always successful, and the supervisor should understand that he cannot automatically blame the steward for frivolous or unjustified grievances. The steward is duty-bound to represent the employee and try to win the grievance. The supervisor should not take the strong advocacy of a fallacious grievance personally.

When representing employees in grievances, stewards have equal standing with management. The law protects stewards from discipline for conduct directly related to grievance processing and enforcement of the contract. The exception is when the steward's conduct exceeds the bounds of "zealous advocacy." For example, stewards are not allowed to threaten supervisors with bodily harm or to physically assault supervisors. They are expected to conduct themselves in a businesslike manner that reflects the decorum customarily found in the work place. Stewards cannot abuse the process by continuously filing frivolous grievances. Otherwise, stewards are granted wide discretion in discharging their union obligations.

In order to discharge the various obligations of his position in the union, the steward is often granted a number of rights over and above those granted to other employees in the bargaining unit. These additional rights have been sanctioned by management and may be included in the contract. Major among these rights is time off to investigate grievances. Some agreements allow leaves of absence to conduct union business. Another common added right given to stewards is super seniority to protect the steward from involuntary transfer or layoff. Each supervisor must have a working knowledge of these special rights granted stewards.

As an employee, the steward must abide by the same work rules as other employees in the bargaining unit. In other words, when not representing employees, the steward must do his job just like any other worker. Stewards should not be allowed to use their position as a representative of the union as an excuse for poor performance. The steward wears two hats — one as an employee and one as a union official. He has an obligation to discharge the responsibilities of both positions.

Good labor relations depend, in large measure, upon the relationship between the steward and the supervisor, because this is where grievances and other disputes usually first come to be settled. The supervisor can and should do a number of things to improve and strengthen this relationship. First, the steward should always be treated with dignity and respect, especially when other employees are present. Supervisors should never purposely embarrass a steward. Such conduct only escalates disputes which might otherwise be minor and settled quickly.

Second, supervisors should never assume that a steward is not sincere in bringing a grievance. The supervisor's attitude toward the steward is normally reflected in the steward's attitude toward the supervisor. This does not mean that the supervisor has to accept as true everything the steward says. When a grievance is submitted, the supervisor shouldn't discredit the steward by telling him, "I don't believe you."

Third, the supervisor should give the steward a chance to retreat from his original position. For example, in a grievance meeting the supervisor should consider restating the contract provision, the common sense involved, the facts in the case and other factors such as past practices. Emphases should be given by the supervisor to those points which the steward did not originally present, which may not have been given to the steward by the grieving employee. This approach allows the steward to consider additional facts and gives him a graceful way out. It is important for the supervisor to remember that it is critical to the steward that the employee being represented feels that an aggressive job of presenting the employee's case to management has been done.

Fourth, supervisors should consult with the steward about significant changes in work rules prior to implementation. The steward should not be surprised by the actions of management. Since the steward is intimately involved in the day-to-day work situation, he may be able to give the supervisor information and points of view not previously considered. The wise supervisor conducts periodic meetings with the steward.

Consultation with the steward is not shared decision making. The supervisor should weigh objectively what he has learned from the steward. If necessary or prudent, the supervisor should then confer with higher levels of management. The final decision is management's. In all cases, the supervisor should report back to the steward regarding the employer's decision and the pending action.

When dealing with stewards, supervisors should not practice management by appeasement or be overfriendly. The supervisor should build a relationship founded on integrity and fairness. The way for supervisors to win respect is to give it.

CHECKLIST
RULES FOR STEWARDS

The union steward is an employee who has been selected to represent fellow workers. Typically, the steward will recruit new members, process grievances, police the contract and act as the union's eyes and ears at the work place. The following rules will usually govern the steward's activities:

_____ 1. When representing employees in grievances, stewards have equal standing with management.

_____ 2. A steward is protected from discipline for conduct directly related to grievance processing and enforcement of the contract, as long as conduct does not exceed the bounds of "zealous advocacy."

_____ 3. When a steward is acting in his own interest, such as presenting his own personal complaint, he is regarded as an employee and not as a union steward.

_____ 4. When a steward has a personal grievance against management, he must follow the grievance procedure established for all employees.

_____ 5. As an employee, the steward must abide by the same work rules as other rank and file employees.

_____ 6. Clearly outrageous conduct by a steward must not be tolerated.

_____ 7. Stewards cannot abuse the process by continuously filing frivolous grievances.

_____ 8. Stewards cannot use their position as representatives of the union as an excuse for poor job performance.

_____ 9. Stewards must follow the established rules when using work time to investigate and process grievances.

STEWARD'S MANUAL*

Introduction

Congratulations on your appointment as a Steward. You hold a demanding and responsible position. You represent a Union that has an impressive list of accomplishments, a forward-looking program and an interest in the welfare of all employees.

Duties of a Steward

1. Recruit New Members

One of your most important duties is to recruit new members. Take advantage of every opportunity to talk about the Union to your fellow workers. Let them know that the Union stands ready to represent individual employees on a legitimate problem that pertains to his work. Remember, "in numbers there is strength." The number of members in the Union determines the amount of service your National Office can give. Increased membership makes possible the hiring of additional representatives to give more and timely assistance to all of our Locals. Be frank when you're talking to prospective members. Don't bluff or misrepresent facts. Promote interest in the Union, and do everything you can under provisions of your contract to encourage membership.

2. Process Grievances

As a Steward, you represent the first-line link between the worker and his Union. He will come to you first with his gripes and complaints. You should be thoroughly familiar with all the grievance procedures available to your members. Be a good listener, but learn to distinguish between petty gripes and legitimate grievances. Be sure you understand the problem and get all the facts. Handle the grievance in a timely manner. Never allow personal beliefs or prejudices to prevent fair handling of any employee complaint. Don't

*This is a synopsis of a number of steward's manuals. Most manuals are far more elaborate, but this version includes the essentials which are a part of virtually all steward's manuals.

pass the buck to other Union Officers when problems come up that should be settled by you. Keep a written record of grievances and your progress in solving them.

3. Render Service

Never take members for granted. Check with them regularly to find out if services given by you and the Union are satisfactory. Anticipate trouble, problems, or dissatisfaction, and move out before a situation develops. Take advantage of every opportunity to offer your assistance without waiting to be called upon. Your actions in providing this kind of unsolicited help may create interest on the part of nonmembers. Never hesitate to contact Officers of your Local to keep them informed of situations which may require their attention or assistance. You are the "eyes and ears" of your Local Union Officers.

Do's and Don'ts for a Steward

As a Union Steward, your duties demand a difficult combination of personal abilities, knowledge, and traits. In the conduct of your day-to-day activities, there are some things that you must do and some you must not do. The following list of do's and don'ts will serve as a guide for you:

DO

1. Know all the provisions of the contract.
2. Get acquainted with the employees in the area you serve.
3. Know all the Officers in your Local and support them.
4. Maintain an "open mind" in dealing with fellow workers.
5. Develop a sympathetic and understanding approach in everyday contacts with employees in your area.
6. Take advantage of every opportunity to become familiar with personnel regulations and local personnel policies.

7. Train yourself to think clearly, find and weigh facts, and be objective.
8. Contact appropriate higher authority, Union or management, when in doubt about issues, procedures, regulations, etc.
9. Be reliable — develop a reputation for getting your work done.
10. Create a good impression of the Union in all your contacts, both with fellow workers and supervisors.
11. Attend all Union meetings.

DON'T

1. Ridicule your fellow workers.
2. Carry a "chip" on your shoulder.
3. Ask for special privileges or consideration merely due to your position as a Steward.
4. Disagree with other Union Officials in front of fellow workers or supervisors.
5. "Pop off" and develop a habit of knocking management unnecessarily or prematurely before you have all the facts and know what you're talking about.
6. Talk too much.
7. Make rash promises which may put you "out on a limb" at a later date.
8. Become satisfied with existing conditions.

SUGGESTIONS TO STEWARDS FOR PRESENTING THE GRIEVANCE

The Problem Of Dealing With Human Beings

1. No two people are approachable in the same manner; this applies to Union members and management officials alike.

2. The Steward is after results that will benefit the worker and the group as a whole; he must suppress personal likes, dislikes, fears and prejudices.

Some Points To Remember When Presenting The Case, Be It Complaint Or Grievance

1. Prepare the Case Beforehand!
   a. Have your facts down in writing.
   b. Have notes organized to guide your presentation.
   c. Anticipate management's argument and have answers ready.
   d. Make an effort to talk to the member or members alone before you meet the supervisor.
   e. Talk the case over, if necessary, with other Stewards, your business agent or others who might help you.
2. Avoid Arguments Among Union People In The Presence Of Management

   If you have a difference of opinion during a meeting, take a recess and iron the problem out in private; present a united front to management!
3. Keep To The Point

   Avoid getting led off on side issues by management.
4. Get The Main Point Of Management's Argument
   a. Try to narrow the area of difference between Union and management.
   b. Try to pin management down on why it did what it did, or failed to do what it should have done.
5. Avoid Getting Excited
6. Treat The Management Representatives As You Would Like To Be Treated
   a. Let any break in good relations come first from the other side.
   b. Remember that the supervisor to whom you are speaking is not always personally responsible for the complaint or grievance; therefore, you may get less

cooperation from him by trying to place the blame on his shoulders.

7. Avoid Unnecessary Delays
   a. If management asks for more time, try to determine whether it is an attempt to stall or is based on a sincere desire for more facts needed to settle the case.
   b. Remember, the more time that passes, the "cooler" the grievance becomes, and the less support you will get from the worker or workers involved.
   c. The longer the complaint or grievance is tied up by management, the more difficult it will be for the Union to gather and remember the facts and merits of the case.
   d. The more grievances that are piled up in the procedure, the more likely that management will try to "horsetrade" settlement of a few grievances for dropping of others.
   e. If the grievances are made a part of contract negotiations, management may attempt to trade off other contract demands for settlement of grievances that should have been taken care of long before.

8. Settle The Grievances At The Lowest Appropriate Step Of The Grievance Machinery — But Make Sure They Are Properly Settled
   a. This saves time.
   b. It helps build better relationships.
   c. The Steward will feel like the vital part of the Union that he is.
   d. Don't pass the buck. If you can settle the grievance satisfactorily in first step, do so.

9. Avoid Bluffing

   It is only a matter of time until your bluff is called. It is wiser in the long run to develop a reputation for honesty.

10. Maintain Your Position On A Grievance Until Proven Wrong

11. Enforce The Contract
    a. If the union has not complained about similar violations of the contract or past practices before, why should management give in now?
    b. The best contract in the world has no value if the workers and stewards do not require management to live up to its terms.

This synopsis of steward's manuals was adapted from training materials developed by the U.S. Department of Labor, Division of Public Employee Labor Relations.

CHAPTER FOUR

What Is A Grievance?

The work place is a fertile breeding ground for many types of complaints and disputes; but not all employee complaints are grievances. Simply stated, a grievance must usually allege that some right guaranteed by the collective bargaining agreement has been violated by the employer.

In labor-management relations most disputes can be categorized as either "rights disputes" or "interest disputes." Generally, "interest disputes" are concerned with the negotiation or modification of the terms of a collective bargaining agreement. They are often unresolved issues in contract negotiations. "Rights disputes," on the other hand, arise during the term of a written agreement and often involve the interpretation and application of that agreement. In a "rights dispute" an employee claims that a legal or contractual right has been violated.

An example of a "rights dispute" would be the case of an employee who is assigned to work 8 hours on Sunday. The Sunday hours are in excess of the employee's regular 40 hours per week, and the employee is paid time and one half for the Sunday hours. The applicable labor contract provision provides that employees who work on Sunday shall be paid double time. A "rights dispute" arises because the employee has a contractual right to the double-time rate. On the other hand, if the union is in negotiations and is attempting to gain a new contract provision granting a double-time rate for all hours worked on Sunday, there would exist an "interest dispute." Instead of a right to double time on

Sunday the employee would have an interest in gaining that right.

It is not uncommon for a union to allege a "rights dispute" to gain changes in conditions of employment that could not be achieved in contract negotiations. Ambiguous contract language, alleged past practices, or an equity claim may be used to pursue a grievance to arbitration for the purpose of gaining some new contractual right for union members. Thus, it is critical that the supervisor be able to distinguish between "interest disputes" and "rights disputes." A supervisor with this skill will enable the employer to successfully resist the gradual expansion of the contract through the grievance procedure.

Fortunately, most collective bargaining agreements contain a well-defined procedure to resolve "rights disputes." Typically, these grievance procedures include a definition of a grievance that both the union and the employer have agreed upon during contract negotiations. It is this more precise definition of grievance or "rights dispute" that the supervisor must thoroughly understand in order to properly handle grievances.

The definition of a grievance does vary a great deal from one labor agreement to another. In some contracts a grievance is very carefully and narrowly defined so as to limit the number of disputes that are subject to the grievance procedure. Other contracts have a broad definition of a grievance resulting in a greater variety of issues that can be pursued through the grievance procedure. There are a great number of labor relations professionals on both sides of the issue of narrow vs. broad definition of grievances. With the give and take of collective bargaining, most labor contracts will have a definition of a grievance that is somewhere between the two extremes.

A very broad definition of a grievance would read as follows:

> "A grievance is any dispute between an employee and the employer."

Obviously, with such a definition no real limitations can be placed on the type of complaints processed through the grievance procedure. Other broad definitions of a grievance will place some restrictions on what can be processed through the grievance procedure. An example of such a grievance definition is:

> "Grievance shall be defined as a dispute between an employee, group of employees, or the union and the employer regarding the application or interpretation of this Agreement or any personnel policy or rule."

This second definition does limit grievances to the contract plus personnel policies and rules.

At the other end of the spectrum is the narrow definition of a grievance. An example is:

> "A grievance is a claim by one or more specifically named employees covered by the provisions of this Agreement that there has been a violation, misinterpretation, or misapplication of a specific written provision of this Agreement which personally and adversely affects the grieving employee or employees."

This definition will limit the number of potential grievances that may be filed under the grievance procedure by creating conditions that must be met in order to be considered as a grievance.

This example of a narrow definition of a grievance imposes the following requirement:

1. The grievants must be specifically named employees. The union cannot file a grievance for unnamed individuals.
2. The grievants must be employees covered by the collective bargaining agreement.
3. There must be an alleged violation, misinterpretation, or misapplication of a specific written provision of the agreement. The grievants must point

out a written provision of the agreement as the basis for the grievance.

4. The violation, misinterpretation, or misapplication of the agreement must personally and adversely affect the employee filing the grievance. The grievant must show personal harm as a result of the employer's action or inaction in interpretation and/or application of the agreement.

The supervisor should insist that the grievant show how he has met all of the conditions required by the definition of a grievance.

The definition of a grievance is often further modified by other provisions of the collective bargaining agreement. One such modification is called an "express waiver" of the right to grieve violations of certain provisions of the contract. An example might be a section in an article dealing with nondiscrimination which reads:

> "Violations of this Article shall not be subject to the grievance procedure set forth in this Agreement."

The purpose of such language is to clearly prevent certain alleged violations of the agreement from being defined as grievances. Such "express waivers" usually occur when statutory or other enforceable procedures are available to redress certain types of employment complaints. The purpose of "express waivers" under these circumstances is to prevent the employee from processing grievances based upon the same set of facts through two or more procedures. In other words, the employee is limited to "one bite at the apple."

It is important that supervisors have a good working knowledge of the definition of a grievance in each collective bargaining agreement they administer. With this skill, a supervisor will know when to raise the defense that a particular grievance is not grievable. Failure to raise this defense in the early stages of the grievance procedure may preclude the employer's advocate from raising that defense in arbitration. This could lead to a gradual broadening of the definition of grievance and other contract provisions by default.

Lawyers and labor relations professionals call this defense "substantive arbitrability." The theory behind this defense is that an employer should not be required to arbitrate a dispute unless the collective bargaining agreement expressly provides for the resolution of such disputes through the grievance and arbitration mechanism. Thus, the employer's advocate will argue that the employer is not obligated to arbitrate a dispute which is not covered by the contract's grievance definition. This creates what is called a "threshold question" which the arbitrator usually resolves by deciding whether or not the subject of the grievance is grievable under the contract.

The concept of "substantive arbitrability" can be explained by the following example:

> The employer and the union have negotiated a narrow definition of grievance as in the example used above. An employee covered by the agreement files a grievance in which it is alleged that the employer has violated the contract by discontinuing a past practice of providing free coffee in the employees' lunchroom. The contract does not refer to the particular past practice nor does it contain a provision requiring maintenance of privileges. In this situation, the employer's representative could challenge the arbitrability of the grievance on the grounds that only grievances as defined by the contract can be arbitrated. Since providing free coffee in the employees' lunchroom is not a specifically written provision of the agreement, the arbitrator will be presented a "threshold question" which must be considered.

In this example, the arbitrator might be asked, "Is the discontinuation of free coffee in the employees' lunchroom grievable?"

Most arbitrators require that employers raise their "substantive arbitrability" defenses during the grievance procedure prior to arbitration. The rationale for this is to prevent the employer from surprising the union with a new defense at the arbitration hearing. This places a burden on supervisors to consider whether or not a grievance is grievable as he prepares his response to the grievant.

It is not wise or a good employee relations practice to respond to all grievances that they are not grievable by definition. Such an approach destroys management's credibility and is looked upon as evidence of bad faith by arbitrators. Each grievance must be reviewed based upon the facts and the presentation made by the employee or his union representative. The following questions have been designed to help determine grievability:

1. Who may file a grievance?
2. May a group of employees file a grievance?
3. May the union file a grievance? If yes, under what circumstances?
4. Must the grievant be adversely affected?
5. Must the grievant claim a specific violation, misinterpretation, or misapplication of the collective bargaining agreement?
6. Are complaints other than violations of the collective bargaining agreement grievable? If yes, what?
7. Is the subject of the grievance barred from the grievance procedure by an express waiver?

The answer to "What Is A Grievance?" is found in the collective bargaining agreement. It is important for each supervisor to understand the working definition of a grievance. Failure can result in an unintentional broadening of the scope of the grievance procedure and the loss of management rights.

CHAPTER FIVE

Preventing Grievances

In a collective bargaining environment grievances are inevitable. Even good supervisors will have to deal with grievances. But there are some proven strategies and techniques supervisors can use to prevent or reduce the number of grievances. Each supervisor should develop and implement a plan to prevent potential grievances.

Grievance processing takes time away from productive work. The steward, grievant and witnesses, if any, will often be pulled off their jobs during the investigation and processing of the grievance. The supervisor will lose valuable time by conducting a grievance meeting, investigating the grievance and preparing an answer. If appealed to higher steps, the lost time is compounded as more levels of management and the union become involved. Thus, a plan to reduce the number of grievances makes good sense.

The supervisor's plan to prevent and reduce the number of grievances should be based on good supervisory practices. Some of the best ways to reduce grievances are listed below.

Know the Contract

Most collective bargaining agreements define a grievance, in part, as "a violation, misinterpretation or misapplication of a provision of the agreement." A foundation for avoiding grievances is for the supervisor to know the contract and to not knowingly violate it. Violations of the contract are a sure way to generate grievances.

The supervisor should first review the contract from cover to cover. After this review the supervisor should study those parts of the contract that can possibly affect his operations. If the supervisor has any questions concerning the intent of any provision of the contract, he should ask the manager responsible for labor relations for clarification. Knowledge of the contract will help eliminate inadvertent violations and reduce the potential for grievances.

Give Clear Communications

A major cause of grievances is the failure of people to communicate. People communicate with each other by means of the spoken and written word as well as by body language. Good communication takes place when the meaning in the sender's mind creates the same meaning in the receiver's mind.

The sender is responsible for insuring that the receiver understands the meaning of his message. Problems arise when the communication has one meaning to the supervisor and a different meaning to the employee. Good communication is mutually understood by both the sender and the receiver.

What is communicated is also determined by the sender's tone of voice, facial expression, body movements and gestures. Words spoken in a loud, angry and aggressive tone will convey a different meaning than the same words spoken in a normal, conversational tone. Tone of voice and body language are often more important than the actual words used. They give insight into the sender's attitude which might alter the meaning of the words and thus transmit a different message.

A shared understanding of the message is critical for effective communications. Expressing feelings, facts or concepts to the supervisor's own satisfaction is not enough. It may not be clear to the employee. The supervisor must take care to make sure what he communicates is not subject to more than one meaning.

The supervisor should check for understanding by asking the employee for feedback. This enables the supervisor to know what message the employee understands. The use of feedback permits the supervisor to modify, adapt, revise or clarify his communication to the employee. This improves the chances that the employee will understand the meaning intended. Feedback is a crucial part of clear communications. Clear communications helps to prevent grievances.

Give Complete Instructions

In addition to clear communications, the supervisor should give complete instructions. When giving employees instructions, supervisors should make sure that their directions are clear and easy to understand. Hurried and incomplete instructions are an invitation for errors. Supervisors should think through instructions before they are given to the employee. As in clear communications, the supervisor should check for understanding by using the feedback technique.

The supervisor must assure himself that the employee knows exactly what he is supposed to do, how he is to perform the work, and the expected results. In some cases the supervisor may need to show the employee where to obtain needed tools, materials, and equipment, provide information and explain the procedures to be followed. With inexperienced employees the supervisor may want to demonstrate or have someone else demonstrate how to do the work. These extra precautions in giving instructions help eliminate misunderstandings between supervisor and employees. Misunderstandings are a major cause of grievances.

Keep Employees Informed

Employees should not hear about the details of their employer's plans from their hairdresser, barber or bartender. They should not be surprised by reading about the employer's plans in the newspaper. Management has an obligation to keep employees informed about the details of changes that will affect them.

Most people prefer face-to-face communications as the source of information. Employees are no different. This was confirmed in 1984 by management consultants Towers, Perrin, Forster and Crosby. They polled 10,000 American and Canadian employees on their current and preferred sources of organizational information. Most employees ranked the immediate supervisor as the preferred source of information.

Employees should be told about any changes planned by management which will affect them. As soon as a definite decision has been made, the supervisor should inform his employees. It is not enough to merely announce the change. Reasons for the change should be explained and employees given a chance to ask questions and get answers.

Informed employees are more productive. Because of this, supervisors should keep employees informed about their jobs, department and employer. By quickly informing employees of pending changes, speculation and rumors can be reduced.

Dispel Rumors

A rumor is unverified information of uncertain origin which is usually spread by word of mouth. Organizational gossip among employees can be very debilitating for the employer as employees spend work time talking and speculating about the latest rumor. Grievances are generated when employees prematurely react based upon a rumor.

Even where supervisors keep employees well informed, rumors will not be completely eliminated. When rumors are detected, supervisors should take prompt action. Giving the employees the facts will dispel most rumors. Taking the initiative in dealing with rumors reduces grievances.

Listen to Employees

Being a good listener is an important supervisory skill. Active listening is hard work. It requires the supervisor to give his undivided attention to the employee and to attempt to understand what is being communicated. Techniques for active listening are outlined at the end of CHAPTER SEVEN.

These techniques will show the employee that the supervisor is interested in the employee's opinions and suggestions.

Listening includes seriously considering the employee's views. This does not mean that the supervisor must agree with the employee. The decision is still the supervisor's to make. The supervisor should inform the employee concerning the results of their conversation. If the supervisor cannot use the employee's suggestions, the employee should be informed along with reasons. In any event, the employee's contribution should be acknowledged.

Be Visible and Accessible

Besides good listening skills, supervisors should be visible and accessible. In their book, In Search of Excellence, Peters and Waterman popularized the term "Management by Walking Around" known as "MBWA." The good supervisor will spend a considerable amount of time walking among employees. During these walk throughs the supervisor should stop and chat with employees. This is prime time in which the supervisor can get to know his employees and listen to them.

While walking through the work area the supervisor should note any problems in the work environment. The supervisor should ask himself questions, such as:

1. Are employees getting the work done?
2. Are employees working well together?
3. Are employees interested in their work?
4. Do employees have proper tools, supplies, and equipment?
5. Do employees receive cooperation from other work units?
6. Is the working environment clean and safe?
7. Does the working environment need improvement; i.e., noise, light, temperature, ventilation, etc.?

If possible, the supervisor should correct any observed problems or irritations.

The supervisor should not only be visible but also approachable. Employees should feel free to bring problems and concerns to the attention of their supervisor. The supervisor who practices "MBWA" and listens to his employees will be able to nip many grievances in the bud. Besides listening, the supervisor should be observant of the work environment.

Know Employees

Supervisors should develop a genuine interest in their employees. They should make it a practice to have personal contact with each employee every workday. While walking about the work area supervisors should visit with each employee. During this short visit, supervisors should inquire about such things as the employee's family members, concerns about the job, vacation plans or hobbies. Supervisors should strive to be friendly without prying or becoming too intimate.

The observant supervisor who knows his employees will be able to detect problems with individual employees. Some of the danger signals that might be noted by the supervisor are:

1. Lack of enthusiasm or interest in work.
2. Excessive griping.
3. Excessive absenteeism, tardiness or loafing
4. Increase in errors.
5. Decline in productivity.
6. Change in physical appearance, such as grooming habits, dress and neatness.
7. Sudden changes in mood, such as overreactions to situations, loud outbursts or sudden depression.

The alert supervisor who practices "MBWA" and knows his employees as individuals should be able to detect these and other danger signals. Early corrective action will eliminate the potential for grievances.

Avoid Favoritism

Favoritism shown by a supervisor is almost certain to cause grievances and other problems in the work place. Inconsistency is a form of favoritism. For example, if the supervisor disciplines one employee for overextending the lunch break but continues to overlook the persistent late return from lunch of another, or the supervisor gives the best overtime opportunities to certain workers, that supervisor is favoring some employees. A supervisor must treat all employees fairly and impartially, and in a consistent manner.

Favoritism unleashes strong emotions in employees such as envy and jealously. If allowed to go unchecked, favoritism will destroy employee morale and respect for the supervisor. Since favoritism is a form of discrimination in that some employees are treated better than others, it will often result in employee actions.

Show Appreciation

According to the famous American author William James, "The deepest principal of human nature is the craving to be appreciated." No one likes to be taken for granted. Employees need recognition for good work. Recognition reinforces or bolsters a person's self image and motivates employees to strive as hard or harder to gain their supervisor's approval.

The power of recognition was aptly interpreted by William Manchester in describing his World War II experience as a foot soldier: "A man wouldn't sell his life to you, but he will give it to you for a piece of colored ribbon." Mark Twain once pointed out the importance of recognition by saying, "I can live for two months on a good compliment." On the other hand, if employees do not receive recognition for efforts to improve, they become discouraged.

Most employees do not mind working hard; but if no one seems to notice, they say, "What's the use?" Once they become discouraged, it is hard to turn them on to the idea that their efforts are appreciated.

Recognition costs little or nothing. It only takes a minute for the supervisor to say to his employee, "That was a great job you did on that report" or "I appreciated how you handled that customer complaint yesterday." Giving deserved praise should become a regular part of the supervisor's daily chat with his employees.

In giving praise supervisors should follow a few simple rules. These rules protect the supervisor's credibility with employees. When giving recognition supervisors must:

1. Take care to ensure recognition is earned. Praise must be honest;
2. Make sure that praise is spontaneous and unsolicited. Employees can tell when praise is superficial or used for ulterior motives;
3. Make sure compliments are specific and tangible; and
4. Do include written commendations or notations on the employee's evaluation following appropriate verbal compliments.

If the employee does something that deserves praise or recognition, the supervisor should let the employee know it. An employee who feels appreciated by his boss is less likely to file grievances.

Keep Promises

Supervisors should be careful about making promises to employees. If promises are made, they should be kept. It might be well for supervisors to live by the old saying: "Never promise more than you can deliver, always deliver more than you can promise." It is better for the supervisor not to promise anything than to break a promise.

Sometimes employees construe general statements by their supervisor as promises. Care must be taken to avoid statements which can be interpreted as promises. For example, the supervisor might say to an employee, "I have been thinking about you for that new job." The employee may honestly believe that his supervisor has made a promise. If the employee is not assigned to the new job, he will feel betrayed by his boss. The employee is now ripe to file a grievance at the first opportunity.

There are many other good supervisory practices, such as developing a good working relationship with the steward, that will help reduce grievances. "Rules for Reducing the Number of Grievances" that follows, along with the strategies and techniques discussed in this CHAPTER, will help supervisors to develop an action plan to reduce and prevent grievances. The supervisor who knows the contract, has good communication and listening skills, practices "MBWA," knows his employees, gives praise and is fair will have fewer grievances and a more productive work unit.

CHECKLIST
RULES FOR PREVENTING GRIEVANCES

In his book, Front Line Supervisor's Labor Relations Handbook, Stephen F. Byrd says, "A grievance may have some basis in fact, or be a figment of someone's imagination, but in either event it must be dealt with, and should not be ignored. The 'mole hill' becomes a 'mountain' very quickly where alleged labor grievances are involved." While there is no magic formula for preventing grievances, the following general rules will help the supervisor:

____ 1. Do not knowingly violate the contract.

____ 2. Honestly let employees know how they are doing on the job.

____ 3. Act quickly to dispel rumors with the facts.

____ 4. Correct minor irritations promptly.

____ 5. Encourage and listen to constructive suggestions.

____ 6. Don't make promises you can't keep. Keep promises you make.

____ 7. Be visible and accessible to employees.

____ 8. Assign work impartially.

____ 9. Explain reasons for directives and assignments.

____ 10. Be consistent. Explain why when deviations must be made.

____ 11. Explain reasons for change.

____ 12. Act as soon as possible on requests from employees.

____ 13. Avoid showing favoritism.

____ 14. When giving criticism or discipline, do it in private.

____ 15. Keep the union steward informed about significant plans.

CHAPTER SIX

The Grievance Procedure

Collective bargaining is not confined to negotiating an agreement every one, two or three years. It is a continuous process. There is no such thing as a complete collective bargaining agreement which covers in detail all the situations that will arise during its term. Thus, labor and management negotiate into the contract a grievance procedure to resolve day-to-day uncertainties. Because of its central role in this continuous process, the grievance procedure becomes the cornerstone of the collective bargaining agreement.

The grievance procedure usually consists of a series of steps or levels to be used within specified time limits. The nature of the grievance procedure will depend upon the structure and type of employer in addition to the needs and desires of management and the union. The typical grievance procedure prescribes a number of appeal steps or levels designed to stimulate dispute resolution at the lowest possible level in the organization. In some cases the parties are unable to resolve the dispute. In anticipation of this problem, over 95 percent of the collective bargaining agreements in the private sector call for binding arbitration as a final step in the grievance procedure. A growing number of grievance procedures in the public sector also end in binding arbitration. Other government sector collective bargaining agreements may use civil service commissions, advisory arbitration, grievance review boards, elected officials or the courts as the terminal step in the grievance procedure.

The obvious purpose of the grievance procedure is to resolve disputes between labor and management over the interpretation and application of the collective bargaining agreement. There are many other less obvious functions of the grievance procedure. Other functions that can be very beneficial to the employer include the following:

- **Dispute Resolution Function**

During negotiations unions will usually give up their right to strike during the life of the contract in exchange for a grievance procedure. The grievance procedure provides an orderly and peaceful method for the enforcement of the agreement. During contract administration the employer administers the contract through interpretation and application. The union polices the contract. If the union disagrees with management's interpretation and application of the agreement, it may use the grievance procedure to enforce the contract. At some point in the grievance procedure the dispute will be resolved.

- **Contract Interpretation Function**

Many provisions of any collective bargaining agreement are not self-explanatory. Contract language will often mean different things to different people. By resolving disputes over the meaning of contract language, the grievance procedure performs a contract interpretation function. The answers to grievances and grievance settlements form precedents that give meaning to contract language. Thus, the contract interpretation function is a guide to the future application of the contract by supervisors.

- **Problem-Solving Function**

Often, specific contract provisions do not adequately address the changing day-to-day needs of the work place. When this occurs, problems develop as to the proper interpretation and application of the agreement. The grievance procedure is a vehicle for problem solving. Each level of management brings additional resources to bear on the problem until it is solved. The solution to the problem will aid the contract interpretation function by creating a new interpretation of the contract.

Communication Function

The grievance procedure is an orderly method employees can use to communicate with management. Because the procedure provides for successive steps up the chain of command, employees and/or their union have a way of informing higher management of problems at the line-supervision level. This "window to the work place" gives upper management an opportunity to audit contract administration by supervisors. The grievance procedure also communicates to management employees dissatisfaction with particular provisions of the collective bargaining agreement. This acts as a "barometer for negotiations," because during negotiations the union will probably seek to change those areas that are aggravating its members.

Safety-Valve Function

When employees are upset over a particular application of the contract by management, the grievance procedure can act as a therapeutic safety valve. By taking the steam out of tense situations, management can avoid work disruptions and aggression directed at the employer. This safety-valve function also allows management to identify problems before they become explosive. Once the problem is identified, it can be peacefully resolved.

Management Improvement Function

The existence of a grievance procedure puts pressure on management to improve internal communications and coordination in contract administration. Regular training and briefings become necessary in order to insure that the contract is interpreted and applied uniformly and consistently. This helps management to avoid the embarrassment of having to overturn decisions of lower-level managers. With a vigilant union policing the contract and a grievance procedure for enforcement, management must keep on its toes. Otherwise, inadequate management practices will be identified, resulting in greivances which can be costly in both money and prestige.

Most grievance procedures contain the following key parts:

1. Definition of a grievance.
2. Definition of grievant.
3. Specific time limits for filing and processing a grievance.
4. Procedural steps or levels for processing a grievance.
5. Terminal or final step.
6. Regulations governing the operation of the grievance procedure.

The specific operation of these key parts to a grievance procedure will vary from contract to contract. Thus, it is very difficult to generalize about the workings of grievance procedures.

Simply stated, a grievance procedure is a system for considering employee grievances by successively higher levels of management. Grievance procedures almost always consist of a series of steps or levels with specified time limits. The procedure will usually cover all employees in the bargaining unit, whether or not they are union members. Supervisors, managers and other employees outside of the unit are not covered by the negotiated greivance procedure. The employer may have established a separate grievance procedure for nonrepresented employees.

The number of steps in a grievance procedure will vary depending on a number of factors such as size and complexity of the organization. Small employers can be expected to have short, simple grievance procedures, sometimes with only a couple of steps. Larger employers usually have four or more steps in their procedure. Large organizations with many departments and multiple work locations may have very long, formal grievance procedures. There is no typical grievance procedure in terms of the number of levels or steps.

Usually, the first step in the grievance procedure is when the employee presents his grievance to his immediate supervisor. This is often called the informal level. If informal, the grievance is presented verbally and the supervisor gives an oral answer. In some procedures all steps, including the first step, are written. Most contracts set a time limit between the alleged violation of the contract and when the employee must activate the first step of the grievance procedure. The purpose of the time limit is to bring about a quick resolution of the grievance and to limit employer liability if money damages are involved.

If the employee does not activate the grievance within the time limits, he may forfeit his rights to have the grievance adjusted. Once exception is in the case of a continuous grievance which is an ongoing violation of the contract as opposed to a single isolated and complete transaction. In a continuous grievance, the violation of the contract is repeated from day to day. In other words, each day there is a new violation of the contract.

The concept of continuous grievance allows the correction of contract violations that first occurred at some time in the past. Examples of disputes which have been held as continuing violations include: improper wage rate, change in commission structure, misassignment of work, misclassification of work, failure to pay proper job rate, job classification, upward reclassification, improper subcontracting and incorrect calculation of seniority. The continuous grievance can be filed at any time without being deemed a violation of the specific time limits stated in the grievance procedure. Usually, back pay, if any, will be limited to the date the grievance was filed. The theory is that the employer should not be liable for the period of time the employee failed to enforce his rights under the collective bargaining agreement.

The doctrine of continuing grievance is frequently misunderstood and misapplied. When confronted with a possible continuing grievance, the supervisor should seek help from upper management. If still in doubt, a good rule of thumb for supervisors is to deny the grievance based, in part, on timeliness.

If the employee is not satisfied with the answer given at step one, he may move the grievance to step two of the grievance procedure. Under most contracts, the employee is the moving party and has the burden to push the grievance through the procedure. If the employee fails to move the grievance to the next level within the prescribed time limits, it is often assumed that the last answer given by management to the grievance was accepted by the employee. If management fails to respond within the time limits, the obligation is usually on the employee to move the grievance on to the next step.

At step two grievances become more formal and are usually transacted in writing. At this point in the grievance procedure, the answers and settlements to grievances will often constitute precedents for future interpretation and application of the contract. Thus, written answers to grievances should be carefully drafted and reviewed by upper management.

Depending upon the negotiated procedure, the employee may pursue his grievance through several more levels until the final step is reached. The final level could be binding arbitration, advisory arbitration, grievance review board, civil service commission, etc. In any event, the collective bargaining agreement is a legally binding contract; thus, in the absence of binding arbitration the employee or his union may, as a final step, file a law suit to enforce the contract.

Most grievance procedures contain a number of regulations governing the operation of the procedure. For example, the grievance procedure may have provisions for extension of time limits. Normally, the time limits can only be extended by written agreement of the parties. Some grievance procedures provide for advance step filing of grievances in certain circumstances. For example, grievances involving the termination of an employee or a grievance involving employees at more than one work location or department may be filed at step two or three. Another common rule found in grievance procedures governs the consolidation of grievances involving the same issue. These regulations are included in the grievance procedure in order to adapt the operation of the procedure to the varied

The supervisor should fully understand his obligations under the grievance procedure and the obligation of the grievant. The "Grievance Procedure Question Guide" and "Grievance Procedure Flow Chart" at the end of this CHAPTER are designed to help supervisors and managers to better understand their grievance procedures. When completed, these aids provide a quick reference when supervisors must answer procedural questions while handling grievances.

The grievance procedure is a negotiated private dispute-resolution system. It serves many beneficial functions during the continuous contract administration stage. Even though there are common key elements, grievance procedures vary greatly in actual operation from contract to contract. In order to effectively handle grievances, supervisors should carefully analyze each grievance procedure they must administer.

HOW TO USE THIS CHART

This chart diagrams the first three steps or levels in a typical grievance procedure. When completed the chart will show critical time limits and other important information about the grievance procedure.

The article in the contract in which the grievance procedure is found is recorded in the space under the heading.

The space between "Incident That Caused Grievance" and "Level I" is used to record the number of days the employee has to file the grievance. The first line under "Level I" is used to record the title of the position that is responsible for processing the grievance at Level I. The next space is used to record whether the answer is oral or written. The final space is used to record the number of days the supervisor has to respond.

The space between "Level I" and "Level II" is used to record the number of days the employee has to appeal a grievance to "Level II." The first line under "Level II" is used to record the title of the position that is responsible for processing the grievance at "Level II." The final space is used to record the number of days the manager has to respond.

The space between "Level II" and "Level III" is used to record the number of days the employee has to appeal a grievance to "Level III." The first line under "Level III" is used to record the title of the manager who is responsible for processing the grievance at "Level III." The final space is used to record the number of days the manager has to respond.

The space at the bottom of the chart is used to record whether time limits are calendar days or workdays.

GRIEVANCE PROCEDURE

(For Details See Article ______ of Contract)

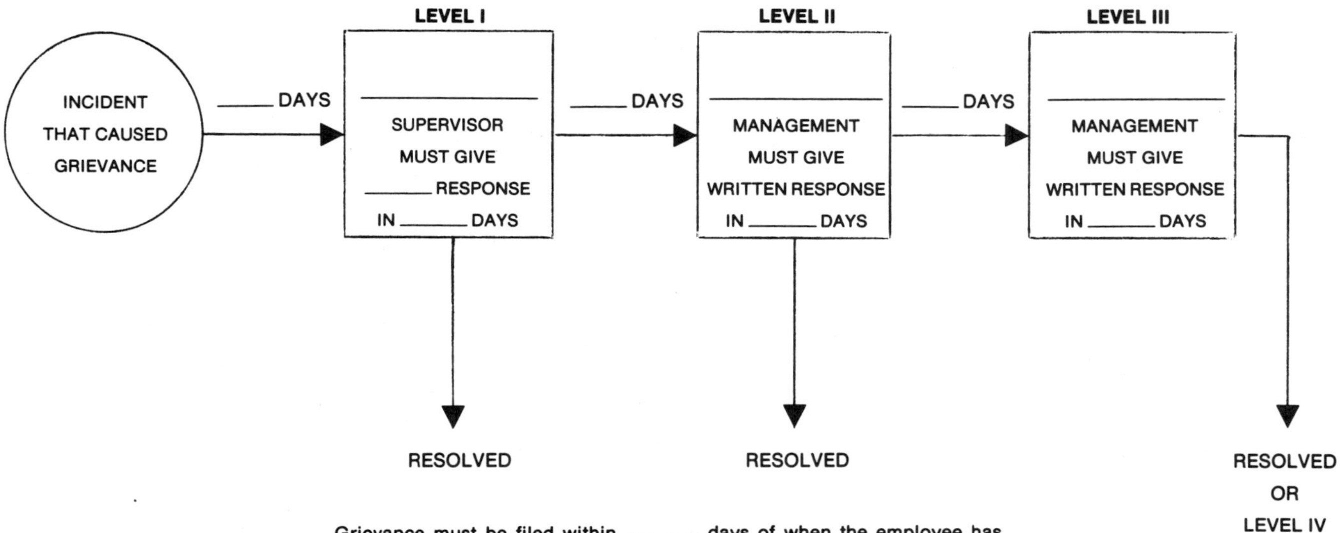

Grievance must be filed within ______ days of when the employee has knowledge of the event that caused the grievance.
Must the grievance be in writing? __________

QUESTION GUIDE
THE GRIEVANCE PROCEDURE

Level One

1. To whom is the grievance presented at Level I?
2. How many days does the employee have in which to present the grievance?
3. Must the grievance be oral or in writing?
4. If in writing, must the grievance be on a grievance form?
5. How many days does management have in which to answer the grievance?
6. Is management's answer written or oral?
7. What happens if management does not answer the grievance?

Level Two

1. To whom is the grievance presented at Level II?
2. How many days does the employee have in which to file an appeal at Level II?
3. Must the grievance be oral or in writing?
4. If in writing, must the grievance be on a grievance form?
5. How many days does management have in which to answer the grievance?
6. Is management's answer written or oral?
7. What happens if management does not answer the grievance?

Level Three

1. To whom is the grievance presented at Level III?
2. How many days does the employee have in which to file an appeal at Level III?
3. How is the grievance presented?

4. How many days does management have in which to answer the grievance?
5. How does management answer the grievance?
6. What happens if management does not answer the grievance?

Final Level

1. Are there other steps prior to the final level? If yes, how many and what are the levels.
2. What is the final step in the grievance procedure?
3. Must the union authorize the final step?
4. How many days does the employee and/or the union have in which to file an appeal at the final step?

Operating Rules

1. Are days calendar days or workdays?
2. Does the procedure allow for extension of time limits?
   How?
3. Does the procedure allow for advance step filing of a grievance? If yes, under what circumstances?
4. Does the procedure allow for consolidation of grievances? If yes, under what circumstances?

CHAPTER SEVEN

How To Process A Grievance

The most important relationship in the work place is that of the employee and the immediate supervisor. Often the supervisor is the only member of management with whom the typical employee has any direct contact. In the eyes of the employee, the supervisor is management. The actions of the supervisor represent the actions of the employer to the employee.

The supervisor directs the day-to-day work of the employee. Often this will include showing the employee how to do the job or making arrangements for someone else to show the employee. The supervisor will monitor and evaluate the performance of the employee. It is the supervisor who should keep the employee informed about activities of management. The supervisor also administers the collective bargaining agreement and insures that the employer's policies and procedures are fairly implemented.

As the supervisor interprets and applies the various provisions of the contract, the potential for conflict is created. One or more employees may feel that the contract was not uniformly or impartially applied. There may be those who feel some right guaranteed by the contract has been violated. In other words, as the supervisor makes those endless day-to-day decisions, there is always the possibility for a grievance.

Even the best supervisors are confronted with employee grievances. Resolving employee grievances is a major responsibility of the supervisor. The attitude which the supervisor displays in handling grievances will often determine whether or not the grievance can be effectively resolved. A defensive attitude toward grievances will only result in increased militancy, poor employee attitudes and loss of morale. Using employee grievances as an opportunity to solve problems will strengthen the supervisor's credibility with the work force.

Most employee complaints go through several phases before they become formal grievances. The first phase usually begins when an employee is irritated by some job-related problem. Perhaps the employee did not get the promotion he wanted, or management changed his work schedule, or the employee may feel that management is showing favoritism in the assignment of overtime work. The possibilities are many. In each case the problem is important to the employee. The skilled supervisor will try to anticipate problems and resolve them before they become formal grievances.

The second phase is when the employee begins to complain about his problem. Often, the upset employee will complain to coworkers or the steward. At this point the employee is trying to gain sympathy and support from others. It is during this phase that the "grapevine" usually tells the supervisor that trouble is brewing. The supervisor should meet with the employee in an attempt to resolve the employee's problem before it becomes a formal grievance.

The final phase is reached when the employee becomes so unhappy that he files a formal grievance. At this point the supervisor is still in a position to resolve the problem if he properly handles the grievance.

In most grievance procedures it is customary for the employee to present his grievance to his supervisor at this first step. The employee may or may not be assisted by a union representative. While there is no magic formula that will guarantee the supervisor will be able to resolve the grievance to the employee's satisfaction, there are certain proven practices that do help bring a resolution.

Grieving employees are often upset and angry. The supervisor must resist the temptation to fight back or become defensive when dealing with an irate employee or belligerent union representative. The supervisor should try to set up an informal atmosphere. Everyone should be comfortably seated in a private room free from distractions. The "Checklist — Rules for Improved Listening" at the end of this CHAPTER is a good guide for conducting grievance meetings.

The supervisor should assure the employee of his concern for the employee's problem. A statement like "I am also concerned about a fair and just resolution to your grievance" is important for setting the right tone.

The supervisor must stay composed and not show any anger or excitement. The supervisor's goal is to observe the three C's: "Be calm, be cool and be collected." Some union representatives will try to bait the supervisor into an angry outburst or admission which can be used against the supervisor in subsequent grievance meetings. Supervisors must resist this old ploy.

Supervisors must let the employee tell his story. Many employees feel that their supervisor never listens to them. The easiest way to resolve many grievances is to "let the employee get it off his chest." Often, employees will drop their grievance after they are allowed to tell their story.

The supervisor should listen carefully and hear the employee out. Even if he disagrees with the employee, the supervisor should not interrupt. It is not necessary for the supervisor to defend himself. The supervisor is there to hear the employee's complaint and to gather facts. The grievant has the burden of presenting reasons and rationale for the grievance. It is best if the supervisor allows the employee to talk as much as he wants. The experience may act as a catharsis, resulting in better feelings and the employee's willingness to accept the supervisor's later response to the grievance.

The supervisor should adopt a problem-solving attitude by asking questions. The best questions cannot be answered by a simple yes or no. The supervisor should ask:

1. Specific questions to get the facts; such as, "On

what day did the incident happen?"

2. Questions that seek additional information; such as, "Can you give me an example of how. . .?"
3. Open-ended questions; such as, "How do you feel about. . .?"
4. Paraphrasing questions; such as, "Are you saying that. . .?"
5. Clarification questions; such as, "What do you mean when you say. . . ?"

Questioning is a powerful tool that should be used to control the grievance meeting and improve listening skills. The "Question Guide for Handling Grievances" at the end of this CHAPTER is designed to help supervisors to ask questions that will make the grievance meeting productive.

Questions are windows to the employee's mind. Often, the grievance is just a symptom of a bigger problem. By questioning the employee, the supervisor may be able to uncover an underlying problem that caused the grievance. When this happens the supervisor is in a better position to deal with the real problem.

Before the grievance meeting is over, the supervisor should take pen in hand and ask the employee to go over the story again while he takes notes. The supervisor should record all the critical facts; including, when, where, why and what. The "Checklist — Processing the Grievance" will aid the supervisor in recording important information. After getting all the facts recorded, the supervisor should then restate the grievant's story and the requested action in his own words. The grievant should be asked to confirm whether or not the supervisor has correctly restated the story. Listening to the grievance restated in someone else's words often gives the employee the chance to evaluate the reasonableness of his grievance. Some employees may withdraw all or part of the grievance after they hear the supervisor restate their grievance. By restating the grievance, the supervisor is guaranteed that he has a clear understanding of the grievance and the remedy desired by the employee.

As the final step in the grievance meeting, the supervisor should assure the employee that he will respond to the grievance within the prescribed time limits. By responding at a later date, the supervisor has an opportunity to investigate the grievance and report his findings to upper management. In addition, the supervisor avoids making a hasty decision under pressure from the employee and his union representative. By waiting, the supervisor minimizes the chance of error and a reversal at a higher step in the grievance procedure.

Following the grievance meeting, the supervisor should investigate the grievance. The first place to start in analyzing a grievance is with the definition of a grievance in the collective bargaining agreement (see "What is A Grievance?"). The supervisor should make sure that the employee's grievance fits the contractual definition. Next, the supervisor should check the grievance procedure for time limits. Most contracts require the employee to file the grievance within a specific number of days from the incident that gave rise to the grievance or when the employee should have reasonably been aware of the grievance. At the same time, the supervisor should check his time limits for responding. After checking the grievance procedure, the supervisor should review the entire contract. Particular attention should be given to all provisions that the employee alleges have been violated and the management rights clause. Established employer practices should also be researched. Practices can often be checked by consulting the manager responsible for labor relations. Other supervisors may be contacted to determine their practices in similar situations.

Often, employer records are important in establishing the facts involved in a grievance. The supervisor may wish to review appropriate records such as time cards, leave requests, accident reports, personnel transactions, etc. The employer's personnel or employee relations office will often help in this effort. The administrator of the employer's labor relations function can provide information on how similar grievances have been settled in the past.

After fully investigating the facts, the supervisor is ready to answer the grievance. A good supervisor will make a preliminary decision and then test the answer with the manager responsible for labor relations. This helps to ensure that the supervisor's decision will be supported by upper management.

In preparing the written answer, the supervisor should respond only to the issues raised in the grievance. Raising new issues will only broaden the scope of the grievance and make it more difficult to resolve. The written response should be very brief and to the point. The grievance response must be signed and dated by the supervisor. The two "Sample Grievance Answers" at the end of this CHAPTER show how the supervisor's response to a grievance should be written.

When the grievance is legitimate, the supervisor should grant the grievance along with a reasonable remedy. Often, just meeting with the employee and candidly admitting the error and assuring that it will not be repeated will resolve the grievance. When management has made a mistake, it is best to admit it and get on with business. Defending an obvious error discredits the supervisor and the employer.

The best way to communicate a negative grievance response to the employee is in a meeting. In a face-to-face meeting, the supervisor is able to explain the reasons for rejecting all or part of the grievance. The supervisor is also in a position to sell the employee on the correctness of the decision. If the employee is still dissatisfied, it is a good practice to explain the grievance procudure so that the employee knows his right to appeal the answer to a higher level. The supervisor should always try to end the meeting on a pleasant note. This can be accomplished by thanking the employee for bringing the problem to the employer's attention and sharing his feelings.

Once the answer has been prepared and given to the grievant, it is important for the supervisor to stick with the decision. At the meeting, the employee or union representative may try to pressure the supervisor into changing his answer. Various tactics may be used, such as threats of appeal. If the supervisor backs down, he will be encouraging more grievances. When the union discovers that the supervisor is unsure of himself or that he gives in under pressure, it knows that it can single him out as the one to file grievances against. After the answer is presented to the employee, any change should be made at higher steps in the grievance procedure.

After the meeting, the supervisor should collect all of his notes and papers and write a grievance record for the file. There is a "Sample Grievance Record" and a "Sample Grievance Record Form" at the end of this CHAPTER. The grievance record, along with other evidence collected by the supervisor, will be needed if the employee appeals the grievance response. On the other hand, if the grievance is settled, the settlement may become a precedent for other grievances in the future that involve the same issues. The passage of time distorts the recollection of what occurred. Thus, a good grievance file containing a complete record of the grievance is a critical strategy for preserving management rights.

If the supervisor grants all or part of the grievance, it is important to follow up to make sure that the promised remedy is granted. Especially in large organizations, communications problems result in either excessive delay or the employee never receives the remedy. This situation will destroy the supervisor's credibility. The supervisor owes it to the grievant and himself to follow through to make sure that the employee received the remedy.

Even if the supervisor correctly follows all of the steps for processing a grievance, there is the chance that the supervisor may be reversed at a higher level. This might be for a number of reasons, including the following:

1. Additional factors might have developed;
2. The supervisor might have slipped up in investigating or in weighing the facts;
3. The supervisor might have misunderstood management's interpretation of the appropriate contract

language;

4. The necessity of changing a previously established policy might become apparent just at the time a particular case comes up for review; or
5. The evidence is not sufficient to convince an arbitrator.

Whatever the reason for reversal, the supervisor should not take it as a personal failure. It should be viewed as an opportunity to learn and sharpen skills for the next grievance.

The supervisor is a key player in the grievance procedure. If the supervisor properly handles grievances, there is less chance that management rights will be eroded away. In addition, the well-conducted grievance meeting will enhance the supervisor's credibility with employees, even when it is necessary to deny the grievance. If a grievance is appealed, the well-written answer and complete grievance record will become critical factors when the grievance is reviewed at higher levels.

CHECKLIST

RULES FOR IMPROVED LISTENING

Most people do not perceive a difference between hearing and listening. Hearing is the physiological process involved in picking up sounds. Listening is making sense of those sounds. Often people hear others speak but never listen to the message they are communicating. The following rules will improve listening skills:

____ 1. Avoid distractions by meeting in a quiet location without interruptions. Don't doodle or play with your pencil or other objects while the employee is talking.

____ 2. Make it easy for the employee to talk. If in your office, get out from behind your desk and make sure everyone is seated comfortably. Smile and make eye contact with the employee.

____ 3. Relax and don't get excited or angry. Observe the three C's: "Be calm, be cool and be collected."

____ 4. Don't interrupt, even if the employee is wrong. Let the employee talk as much as he wants.

____ 5. Listen carefully with an open mind — don't defend yourself or prepare counter arguments.

____ 6. When the employee stops talking, don't immediately begin speaking. A short pause may encourage the employee to present more information.

____ 7. Ask questions to gather facts and to understand the grievance.

____ 8. Give feedback to show the employee that you are listening and are interested. Use responses such as "Oh!" "I see." "Really?" or "Uh-huh."

____ 9. Repeat the grievance and the essential facts in your own words to ensure that you understand the grievance.

____ 10. Listen for the real grievance. Often there are underlying problems. As you listen, ask yourself, "What is the real complaint?"

_____ 11. Empathize with the employee. Try to put yourself in the grievant's situation so that you can see his point of view.

QUESTION GUIDE FOR GRIEVANCE HANDLING

"Questions are windows to the mind" *

Questioning is the most powerful tool management has in controlling a grievance meeting. By skillful questioning, management can show interest in the employee's grievance. Often an employee is satisied just to have someone in management listen and show concern about his complaint. The following are some questions which may be helpful in conducting a grievance meeting:

1. Tell me more about that situation?
2. Can you give me another example?
3. I'm not sure I understand. Can you explain that to me?
4. What do you mean when you say equity problem?
5. Has this happened to anyone else? Who?

What are some other potentially good questions to ask during a grievance meeting?

1.
2.
3.

* From Gerard I. Nierenberg, Fundamentals of Negotiating, Hawthorn Books, Inc. New York

CHECKLIST
PROCESSING THE GRIEVANCE

FIRST: GET THE FACTS!

You must know who, when, where, why and what is involved in the grievance. Then wait until you are sure of the answer before you respond.

____ 1. WHO: Name of employee.

Name of the employee's grievance representative.

Names of witnesses, if any.

____ 2. WHEN: Date of incident.

Time of incident.

Time limits (was grievance filed within time limits).

____ 3. WHERE: Place incident happened.

____ 4. WHY: Why did it happen?

a. Employee's contention.

b. Management's contention.

____ 5. WHAT: What happened (statement of incident or problem)?

What is involved (the issue)?

What resolution is sought?

What evidence do you have?

What section of the Contract was allegedly violated?

____ 6. WAIT: Check the contract, rules & regulations.

Check policies and practices.

Check with your superior.

Check with manager in charge of labor relations.

SAMPLE
GRIEVANCE FORM

NAME N. O. Class

WORK LOCATION George Meany High School

JOB TITLE Classroom Teacher

UNION REPRESENTATIVE: RUTH LESS

ARTICLE(s) & SECTION NUMBER(s) Article XV, Section 2

STATEMENT OF GRIEVANCE: I have 28 students enrolled in my wood shop class. There are only 25 complete work stations. Article XV, Section 2 of the Contract requires that "Student enrollment should not exceed number of work stations. . ."

RESOLUTION OR REMEDY SOUGHT: Immediately reduce the class size of my wood shop class to not more than 25 students.

DATE May 16, 1987 SIGNATURE ________

IMMEDIATE SUPERVISOR'S RESPONSE: There are 28 work stations made up of tables and stools. The grievance is untimely, enrollment in class has been at 28 since the third week of September, 1986. The language of Article XV, Section 2 is permissive, not mandatory. Past practice is to enroll 28 students in wood shop.

DATE Feb. 13, 1987 SIGNATURE ________

Distribution of Copies:

White — Immediate Supervisor　Green — Grievant
Pink — Director, Employee Relations　Goldenrod — Union Representative

SAMPLE
GRIEVANCE FORM

NAME O. T. Gripe

WORK LOCATION Building Services Department

JOB TITLE Plumber

UNION REPRESENTATIVE: TY RADE

ARTICLE(s) & SECTION NUMBER(s) Article XII, Section 5

STATEMENT OF GRIEVANCE: I should have been placed on the overtime work list on November 11, 1985. I have not received equal overtime as required by Article XII, Section 5.

RESOLUTION OR REMEDY SOUGHT: Pay for three hours overtime on November 11, 1985, at the rate of time and one half. In addition, assignment to available overtime on November 14, 1985.

DATE Nov. 14, 1985 SIGNATURE ____________

IMMEDIATE SUPERVISOR'S RESPONSE: Grievant was offered overtime on September 1, September 15, October 4, and October 12, 1985, and turned it down. If he had accepted overtime on those days, he would be equal with the other employees in his classification. Finding no violation of Article XII, Section 5, this grievance is denied.

DATE Nov. 17, 1985 SIGNATURE ____________

Distribution of Copies:

White — Immediate Supervisor Green — Grievant
Pink — Director, Employee Relations Goldenrod — Union Representative

SAMPLE
GRIEVANCE RECORD

DATE:	November 17, 1985
EMPLOYEE (S) INVOLVED:	O. T. Gripe
UNION REPRESENTATIVE:	TY RADE
EMPLOYEE'S COMPLAINT:	Gripe and Rade came into my office on 11/14 at 8:30 a.m. and complained that Gripe should have been placed on the 11/11 overtime work list. Rade said that Gripe had not been getting equal overtime along with other employees as required by the contract.
REMEDY SOUGHT:	Gripe wants to be assigned to overtime tonight. Rade agreed, but thought Gripe should also get some money for the overtime lost.
ALLEGED VIOLATION OF:	Article XII, Section 5 — AFSCME Agreement
GRIEVANCE FILED WITHIN TIME LIMITS:	Yes.
FACTS INVESTIGATED:	I reviewed my files and found that Gripe was given equal chance at overtime, but turned it down on 9/1, 9/15, 10/4 and 10/12. If he had accepted overtime on those days, he would be equal with other employees in his classification.
ANSWER GIVEN:	I met with Gripe and Rade on 11/17 at 8:30 a.m. and reviewed times that Gripe had turned down overtime. Told Rade I had to deny the grievance. Rade said that they would think about it.
ACTION TAKEN:	Grievance was denied.
FOLLOW-UP:	None, except to work with Gripe on future overtime assignments so he knows he is getting equal chance.

SAMPLE
GRIEVANCE RECORD FORM

Date: ______________________ Labor Relations Notified: ______________

Employee(s) Involved: ____

____

Union: ________________________ Representative: ________________

- -

Complaint:

____

____

____

____

Remedy Sought:

____

____

____

____

Alleged Violation of: ______________________________________

____

____

Filed Within Time Limits: ___________________________________

____

Facts Investigated: ____

____

____

____

Response to Grievant: ______________________________________

____

____

____

Action Taken: ____

____

____

____

Follow-up: ____

____

CHAPTER EIGHT

Criteria For Contract Interpretation

Over the years labor relations practitioners and arbitrators have developed a number of basic criteria or standards for contract interpretation. The goals of these criteria or standards is to determine the mutual intent of management and labor when the contract was negotiated. A general understanding of the basic rules of contract interpretation will assist the supervisor in day-to-day contract administration and grievance handling. But there is no scientific formula applied to the criteria for contract interpretation by which a supervisor can always predict a particular arbitrator's award in a specific case.

The person in the organization responsible for the overall administration of the collective bargaining agreement is a valuable resource who should be tapped when an interpretation is needed. Only the most basic rules of contract interpretation are presented here. It takes many years of training and experience to develop an in-depth working knowledge of all the rules of contract interpretation and the frequent exceptions to the rules.

Clear and Unambiguous Language

Ambiguous contract language is capable, under a certain set of facts, of having more than one meaning. In other words, the contract language at issue is subject to various interpretations. When contract language at issue in a grievance is "clear and unambiguous," only one interpretation can be applied to the language. It is the "clear and unambiguous" language test that prevails over all other criteria in contract interpretation.

Even though language in a collective bargaining agreement may be "clear and unambiguous," grievances may still arise over that language. This happens because the union may be pressured into pursuing a grievance or because of a lack of understanding on the part of the union or some of its members. Even though management and labor disagree as to the meaning of contract language, an arbitrator who finds the language to be unambiguous will enforce the clear meaning.

Specific v. General Language

It is very common for a subject to be covered in some way by two or more contract provisions. When this occurs and there is conflict between specific language and general language in an agreement, the specific language will prevail. An example of this situation would be a contract which provides, in part:

> "Seniority shall be defined as total years of service with the employer."

A layoff occurs, and a grievance is filed over the method used for calculation of seniority because the employee laid off has more years of service based on hire date. The layoff provision reads, in pertinent part:

> "For purposes of this layoff procedure, employees shall be laid off in order of fewest paid days of service."

The latter more specific language dealing with order of layoff will normally prevail over the more general language found elsewhere in the contract defining seniority.

Words Will be Judged by Their Context

Context is that part of a written or spoken statement in which a word of passage at issue occurs. The words and punctuations leading up to and following the word or words at issue will often determine the meaning of the expression. It is possible to give definite meaning to ambiguous or doubtful words by construing them in light of their context. In other words, contract language will gain its meaning by the words with which it is found. Arbitrators call this "construction in light of context."

Normal and Technical Usage of Words

Normally, words and phrases will be defined based upon their common meaning as opposed to some special meaning which either management or labor try to give to them. Thus, many arbitrators have turned to Webster's or some other reliable dictionary in order to find the usual and ordinary definition of disputed terms. Therefore, any term not characteristically a trade or technical term will be construed in its normal or common meaning unless the context or other evidence indicates that a technical meaning was intended by the parties during collective bargaining.

Special trade or technical terms will be interpreted in a trade or technical sense unless clearly used otherwise. Labor relations terms used in an agreement will usually be given their usual and customary labor relations meaning. Special dictionaries for that industry and a labor relations dictionary such as Robert's Dictionary of Industrial Relations may be used in such instances.

In contract interpretation, a well recognized rule of construction is that a word used in the contract in one sense is to be interpreted as used in the same sense throughout the contract. An exception would be if the language of the agreement indicated that a different meaning should be used. Supervisors should also note that the use of two different terms might be found to imply different meaning.

Agreement to be Construed as a Whole

All parts of the collective bargaining agreement convey some meaning or the parties would not have included them in the contract. If contract language is ambiguous, and one interpretation of the language would give meaning and effect to another provision of the agreement while the other interpretation would nullify or render meaningless some other provision, an arbitrator will usually use the interpretation which would give effect to all provisions. Thus, the meaning of each word, sentence, or paragraph must be determined in relation to the contract as a whole.

To Express One Thing is to Exclude Another

To mention one item of a group or class of items without mentioning others may be construed to mean that all others were deliberately excluded. For example, most contracts with teacher unions also cover other bargaining unit members; such as, counselors, resource teachers, psychologists and nurses. If the applicable contract language in question states:

> "Classroom teachers shall attend the back-to-school night and open house at their respective schools,"

then the other bargaining unit members are excluded from the requirement to attend "back-to-school night" and "open house," because they were deliberately excluded when the term "classroom teachers" was specifically included without mentioning other bargaining unit members.

Doctrine of Ejusdem Generis

Under the doctrine of ejusdem generis, general words following an enumeration of specific terms will be interpreted to include only items of the same general nature or class as those enumerated. A common example is the phrase "and other duties as assigned" found in job descriptions. In the case of a secretary, the duties may be enumerated as: "Typing, filing, taking dictation, and answering the telephone." Under the doctrine of ejusdem generis, other duties as assigned must relate to the enumerated duties; i.e., taking notes at meetings, making photocopies, scheduling appointments, etc. Other related duties would not include washing windows and cleaning toilets.

The exception to the doctrine of ejusdem generis arises when one of the parties is able to show that a wider interpretation was intended when the language was negotiated. Past practice, precontract negotiations, industry practice, and other criteria for contract interpretation can be developed to show that the contract should be interpreted to allow for a broader interpretation of what is related to enumerated items.

In Light of the Law

Whenever two or more intepretations of a collective bargaining agreement are possible, the one making the agreement conform to the law will be selected over interpretations that will make the agreement unlawful. It will usually be presumed by arbitrators that labor and management intended a valid contract that conforms with law.

Avoidance of Harsh, Absurd, or Nonsensical Results

When one interpretation of ambiguous contract language would lead to harsh, absurd, or nonsensical results, while an alternative interpretation would lead to fair and reasonable results, the latter interpetation should be used. It will normally be presumed that the parties did not intend for the contract language to produce bizarre results. This will especially be true if one of the parties is seriously affected by an interpretation of ambiguous language that leads to harsh, absurd, or nonsensical results.

Precontract Negotiations

Meaning can be given to ambiguous language by what was discussed by the parties leading up to that language. The minutes or records created during the negotiations can serve as a guide as to the intent of the parties when the disputed language was created. In some cases, the oral testimony of the participants in negotiations may be relied upon by arbitrators.

Customs and Past Practice

The actions of the parties under a collective bargaining agreement will serve as a guide to contract interpretation. Past practice will normally not be considered if the language is "clear and unambiguous." In order for a custom or past practice to exist, the provision of the collective bargaining agreement in question must be consistently and uniformly applied in the same way to the same problem or issue over a length of time so as to lead to the reasonable expectation that such application of the agreement represents the mutual intent of the parties. The "Question Guide for Determining Past Practice" included at the end of this CHAPTER will help supervisors determine if an enforceable past practice exists.

Prior Settlements

Prior settlements to grievances between the employer and the union may be a key to mutual intent. In many situations, such prior settlements represent binding precedents for the interpretation of the contract. Supervisors should check with the person responsible for overall administration of the collective bargaining agreement to find out if there are any prior settlements of grievances involving the same contract language at issue in a grievance. A determination also has to be made to find out if the prior settlement has any precedential value.

Industry Practice

Over the years, each industry has developed certain customs or practices that are common. These customs prevalent in an industry can be used to shed light on ambiguous contract language. It should be noted that a custom or past practice of a particular employer will usually control in case of a conflict with an industry custom or practice.

There are other criteria that have been developed over the years to give meaning to collective bargaining agreements. Regardless of the criteria, it takes much experience and training to analyze criteria and apply it to a specific fact situation. Paul Prasow and Edward Peters said it well in their book, Arbitraton and Collective Bargaining. "A note of caution, however: These standards should serve as guides and not become rigid, undeviating blueprints to be followed as methodically as though labor relations were an exact science. They should never supplant human relations, human judgment, at the job level."

The chart, "Criteria for Contract Interpretation" and "Question Guide for Contract Interpetation," were designed to aid supervisors in interpreting contract language. The "Question Guide for Determining Past Practice" can be applied by supervisors to any factual situation to determine if a past practice exists and the extent of the past practice. Though helpful, these aids are not substitutes for an expert interpretation from an attorney or labor relations professional.

HOW TO USE THIS CHART

This chart shows criteria used to interpret contract language. The purpose of the criteria is to determine the mutual intent of labor and management when the language was negotiated. In other words, the criteria will help determine what the parties intended the agreement to mean when they wrote it.

The Chart works outward. The more important criteria, the closer it is to the center. Clear and unambiguous language is presented at the center of the chart because it is the most important criteria. If the contract language in question is ambiguous, the criteria in box "B" is applied. If the criteria in box "B" does not clear up the meaning of the language, the criteria in the other boxes are applied by working towards the outer edge of the chart.

Even experts who interpret collective bargaining agreements for a living, such as arbitrators, will weigh the criteria differently. This chart shows the process the arbitrator or others will use in evaluating disputed contract language.

NOTE: This chart was adapted from training materials developed by the American Arbitration Association.

CRITERIA FOR CONTRACT INTERPRETATION

E. Judgment

D. Industry Practice

C. Past Practice

1. Length of time.
2. Frequency
3. Consistent and uniform application.
4. Leading to reasonable conclusion.
5. Mutuality.

B. Ambiguous Language — Interpreting the Language of the Contract

1. In light of the law.
2. Specific v. general.
3. Construe as whole.
4. Word context.
5. Avoiding harsh, absurd, nonsensical results.
6. Precontract negotiations.
7. Prior settlements.
8. Against party selecting language.
9. Expressing one thing. to exclude another.
10. Ejusdem generis.
11. Experience and training of negotiators.

A. Clear and Unambiguous Language

F. Other Criteria

1. Avoidance of penalty.
2. No consideration of compromise offers.

QUESTION GUIDE FOR CONTRACT INTERPRETATION

This question guide to contract interpretation is not all inclusive, but it will be helpful for the majority of contract interpretation questions faced by supervisors.

The most effective use of the question guide is in preparation for conference with the person responsible for the overall administration of the labor contract. In other words, the question guide is not a substitute for consultation, but an aid to organize and prepare so that all important points are covered.

1. Is the language in dispute clear and unambiguous? If not, what possible interpretations exist under the facts in the grievance?
2. Is there specific language in the agreement covering the issues in dispute? If yes, what is the language?
3. Is there a special definition that should be given to the language at issue? If yes, what documents or resource materials support the special definition?
4. Does the normal and customary usage of the term give the correct meaning to the language in dispute? If yes, which dictionary definitions best support this position?
5. Does the interpretation given to the language in dispute nullify or render meaningless other provisions of the agreement? If yes, which provisions and how?
6. Does the language in dispute express one thing and exclude others? If yes, how can this be shown?
7. Does the issue in dispute relate to an enumeration of specific terms? If yes, does the issue involve an item of the same general class or type?
8. Does one of the interpretations of the language in dispute produce a harsh, absurd or nonsensical result? If yes, how can this be shown or demonstrated?
9. Does the interpretation of the language rest upon precontract discussions? If yes, are there any notes, records,

letters or other documentation that will clarify the language in dispute?

10. Does the contract provision in dispute involve any legal questions? If yes, what specific statutes, rules or decisions are involved?
11. Is there a past practice involved in the interpretation of the language? If yes, how long has the practice been in effect, and how frequently has it been applied?
12. Have there been prior settlements involving the language at issue? If yes, what is the practice, and how can it be shown?
13. Are there any industry practices that impact the language in dispute? If yes, what is the practice, and how can it be shown?

QUESTION GUIDE
TO DETERMINE PAST PRACTICE

Often past practice is used to interpret ambiguous contract language or where the contract is silent. In order to determine if a past practice exists, the following criteria will be evaluated by arbitrators.

1. Does the practice concern a significant condition of employment?
2. Was the practice established unilaterally by the employer?
3. How long has the practice been in effect?
4. What is the frequency or repetition of the practice?
5. Has the practice been applied consistently and uniformly over time?
6. Do the employees rely upon the practice?
7. Did either management or labor try to incorporate the practice during negotiations?
8. Did either management or labor try to eliminate the practice during negotiations?
9. Were both management and labor aware of the practice? Did both management and labor give their tacit agreement to the practice?
10. Have the underlying circumstances for the practice changed?
11. Does the practice lead to a reasonable conclusion?

CHAPTER NINE

Just Cause

What is just cause? Most private sector and many public sector collective bargaining agreements provide that the employer may discipline employees for just cause; yet these same agreements seldom contain a definition of just cause. To fill this void, a common law definition of just cause has evolved since the 1930's from many different discipline cases decided by arbitrators. The most often cited arbitration is Enterprise Wire Company and Enterprise Independent Union decided by Professor Carroll R. Daugherty on March 28, 1966 (46-LA-363). In that arbitration award, Professor Daugherty set out a list of guidelines or criteria that can be applied to the facts of any employee discipline case. His criteria was framed as a series of seven questions, which is today known as the seven tests for just cause. A "no" answer to one or more of the questions will usually mean that the employer's disciplinary decision contained one or more elements of arbitrary, capricious, unreasonable, or discriminatory action to such an extent that it can be found that management abused its discretion. Therefore, the arbitrator is free to substitute his judgment for that of the employer.

The seven tests are applied to the employer's conduct in making the disciplinary decision prior to the employee's appeal to arbitration. Good documentation completed at each step of the disciplinary process is a vital part of the employer's strategy to meet the "just-cause" tests.

Arbitrator Daugherty's seven tests for "just cause" as refined by other prominent arbitrators are as follows:

1. Did the employer give to the employee forewarning or foreknowledge of the possible or probable disciplinary consequences of the employee's conduct?

   The forewarning may have been given either orally or in writing. Typically, this will consist of actual communication of rules and penalties for violations through staff meetings, posted bulletins, employee handbooks, etc.

   An exception is in cases of serious breach of conduct by the employee. This is because certain offenses, such as insubordination, coming to work intoxicated, drinking intoxicating beverages on the job, or theft of employer's property, are so serious that any employee should know that such conduct is offensive and subject to heavy discipline. Thus, a "no" answer to the questions in such cases does not mean the employer acted without "just cause."

2. Was the employer's rule or managerial order reasonably related to the employer's business and the performance that the employer might properly expect of the employee?

   The rule "obey now, grieve later" will generally be enforced by an arbitrator. If an employee believes that a rule or order is unreasonable, he must nevertheless obey it, unless he sincerely feels that to obey the rule or order would seriously and immediately jeopardize his personal safety or that of others. Employees may refuse to carry out a directive that would require them to commit a crime. In all other cases the employee must obey the rule or directive and file a grievance or complaint after the fact.

3. Did the employer, before administering discipline to an employee, make an effort to discover whether the employee did, in fact, violate or disobey a rule or order of management?

This is the employee's "day-in-court" principle. An employee has the right to know, with reasonable precision, the specific offense with which he is being charged so as to prepare a response or defense.

The employer's investigation must normally be made and completed before its disciplinary decision is made. In other words, the employer will not normally be allowed to dig up additional evidence to prove the employee's guilt after discipline has been taken. The employer must conduct itself like a court and fairly weigh the evidence before taking disciplinary action.

Obviously, there are situations where management must act immediately in response to the employee's behavior. In such cases the proper action is to suspend the employee pending investigation. Following the completion of the investigation, the employer may impose discipline or, if the employee is found innocent, reinstate the employee with full back pay and benefits.

The employer's investigation should include an inquiry into possible justification for the employee's alleged violation of rules or directives. Thus, it is important to hear from the employee and have his response included as part of the investigation. A detailed statement must be taken from each witness and the employee. This documentation is critical in showing that "just cause" existed for the disciplinary action.

4. Was the employer's investigation conducted fairly and objectively?

   At the investigation, the management official may be both "prosecutor" and "judge," but may not also be a witness against the employee. In order to avoid this problem, it is essential for some higher, detached management official to assume and conscientiously perform the role of "judge." In other words, a higher management official not involved in the case should, after a complete review of the case, make the final decision on whether or not to impose discipline.

   In some disputes between an employee and management person there are no witnesses to the indicent other than the two immediate participants. In such cases it is particularly important that the management official acting as "judge" question the management participant rigorously and thoroughly. The record of the investigation should reflect fairness and objectivity.

5. At the investigation, did the management official acting as "judge" obtain substantial evidence or proof that the employee was guilty as charged?

   It is not necessary that the evidence be conclusive or "beyond all reasonable doubt," but the evidence must be truly substantial and not flimsy. The employer must take steps to conduct a full investigation using all available witnesses and other relevant information. Selective use of witnesses and information will only hurt the employer's case if brought out in the hearing.

6. Has the employer applied its rules, orders, and penalties evenhandedly and without discrimination to all employees?

A "no" answer to this question usually results in a finding of discrimination and the negation or reduction in the penalty imposed by the employer.

If the employer has been lax in enforcing its rules or orders, the problem can be remedied by giving fair notice that in the future rules and orders will be rigorously enforced. In this way, the employer can avoid a finding of discrimination in the enforcement and administration of rules and orders.

7. Was the degree of discipline administered by the employer in a particular case reasonably related to (a) the seriousness of the employee's proven offense and (b) the record of the employee in the service with the employer?

A trivial proven offense does not merit harsh discipline unless the employee has properly been found guilty of the same or similar offenses a number of times in the past. There is no specific number of previous minor offenses necessary in order to justify harsh discipline such as dismissal. Reasonable judgment must be used.

The employee's disciplinary record of previous offenses may never be used to discover whether he is guilty of the immediate or latest offense. The only proper use of the disciplinary records or prior offenses is to help determine the severity of discipline once the employee has properly been found guilty of the immediate offense. If two or more employees are guilty of the same offense, their respective work records provide the only proper basis for "discriminating" among them in the administration of discipline. In other words, if three employees are caught engaging in horseplay and two of the three have had previous disciplinary problems while one has had a clean work record (absent any prior disciplinary action), then a harsher disciplinary penalty can be imposed on the two employees with prior disciplinary problems. This would not consititute true dicrimination.

If all of the first six questions are answered "yes" and it is proven that the employee committed a serious offense, such as drunkenness on the job, can a long, continuous, and unblemished work record with the employer be deemed as an abuse of discretion in a discharge case? According to Arbitrator Daugherty, usually "no." Leniency is the prerogative of the employer rather than of the arbitrator, and the arbitrator is not supposed to substitute his judgment in this area for the employer unless there is compelling evidence that the employer abused its discretion. But, a good number of arbitrators will tend to support a good argument to overturn harsh discipline, such as dismissal, based upon many years of employment and spotless work record.

The answers to Arbitrator Daugherty's seven questions in any particular case are to be found in the evidence presented during the arbitration hearing. In some cases the arbitrator may find one or more "no" answers too weak and the other "yes" answers so strong that he may uphold discipline, but reduce the penalty. For example, a discharged employee may be reinstated without back pay. Most arbitrators use the seven tests for "just cause" as a general guideline which they will modify to fit the unique facts of the case to be decided.

The facts in a particular case will be such that the seven tests for "just cause" cannot be applied with scientific precision. The key to meeting the "just cause" tests is to impose discipline for sound job-related reasons with fairness and consistency. Since management's actions in handling a disciplinary case may be reviewed by an outside party, it is important to document each step so as to show how "just cause" was followed by an employer prior to taking final disciplinary action.

QUESTION GUIDE
TO DETERMINE "JUST CAUSE"

This QUESTION GUIDE is a quick and simple method to determine if the elements of "just cause" are present in an employee discipline case.

1. Was the employee aware of, or should have been aware of, the rule, order or expected conduct?
2. Was the employee aware of, or should have been aware of, the disciplinary consequences of his behavior, conduct, or performance?
3. Was the employer's rule or managerial order reasonably related to the orderly, efficient, and safe operation of the employer's business?
4. Was management's directive lawful?
5. Did management conduct a fair and objective investigation before disciplining the employee?
6. Was the employee given an opportunity to be heard and explain his actions prior to the disciplinary action?
7. Did the investigation produce substantial evidence or proof that the employee was guilty as charged?
8. Taking into consideration the employee's previous work record, was the disciplinary action consistent with that imposed against other employees in similar situations?
9. Was the penalty imposed reasonably related to the seriousness of the offense when viewed along with the employee's work record?

A "yes" response to all of these questions would indicate that the employer is able to meet the test of "just cause" if a disciplinary action is challenged.

CHAPTER TEN

Testifying At A Hearing

Most grievance procedures provide for a formal hearing before an arbitrator or some other outside third party. Usually, these hearings are conducted in much the same manner as proceedings in a courtroom. Some of the technical rules and procedures will not be as rigid and formal as in a court of law. But, from the supervisor's perspective it may appear to be a very formal hearing, complete with direct examination by the employer's advocate and cross-examination from the union's representative.

In a grievance hearing, the supervisor is frequently called as a witness. More often than not, it is the supervisor who is management's key witness. Thus, the employer's case may be won or lost based upon the supervisor's performance on the witness stand. The arbitrator or person sitting in judgment will be judging the supervisor's honesty and credibility as a witness. In grievances where there is conflicting testimony between the employer's witness and the union's witness, this perception of honesty and credibility may very well be the deciding element as to the final outcome of the grievance.

The following factors are often used to determine the credibility of a witness:

1. Demeanor while testifying, including appearance, gestures, voice, and attitude, often will influence the arbitrator's decision on credibility of witnesses. The absence or presence of symptoms associated with deception and lying, including restlessness,

changes in complexion, avoidance of eye contact, excessive swallowing, and evasive or vague answers, will often be observed and noted by the arbitrator.

2. The witness' perception of events related to the grievance will be evaluated by the arbitrator. Perception is the process of receiving information through the sense organs; i.e., sight, hearing, smell, taste, and touch. Perception requires mental interpretation of the information received by the sensory organs. Thus, other factual details, such as eye defects, lighting, wind direction, etc., may have a bearing on the witness' perception and credibility. For example, if the witness states that he recognized the grievant as the person present at the time and location involved in the grievance, such testimony would be very persuasive. That credibility can be diminished if it is established that the witness did not previously know the grievant, yet recognized him on the date in question from a distance of over 150 feet in poor lighting. The witness in the best position to accurately hear or see the event in question will have greater credibility.

3. The witness' memory or recollection of the events in the grievance will be evaluated in terms of the general human experience to recall events after the passing of time. It is well recognized that the ability to recall an incident decreases over time. Other factors, including emotional state of witness, age of witness, and health of witness, can have an impact or memory.

4. The witness' reputation for honesty and veracity will usually influence his credibility. A witness with a reputation for honesty can be expected to be more credible than a witness who has a reputation for dishonesty and untruthfulness.

5. The witness with a consistent story from the initial investigation through to final testimony will tend

to be more credible than a witness with an inconsistent story that has changed one or more times.

6. This witness' testimony that is supported by all the established facts of the case will have greater credibility than the witness' testimony that contradicts one or more established facts.
7. The bias, interest, or motive of the witness may have an influence on the arbitrator when he assesses credibility. A witness with an interest in the outcome of a hearing may be less credible than a witness with no personal stake in the final decision.

Most employer advocates will spend considerable time preparing the supervisor for the hearing. This will usually include a review of all the questions that the employer's advocate plans to ask during the hearing. Questions that may be asked by the union's representative should also be reviewed. Since it is impossible to anticipate all questions that may be asked during the hearing, the supervisor should have an understanding of the theory of the case and how his testimony will be tied into the case.

Many employers have developed a set of written instructions for witnesses. These instructions are given to the witness prior to the hearing for his study and review. The following is a sample set of instructions for witnesses:

SAMPLE
INSTRUCTIONS FOR WITNESSES

You have been called to testify in a hearing for your employer. The issues involved in this hearing are important to your employer. Your role in this process is to provide truthful and accurate answers to questions. In answering the questions, your credibility as a witness will be judged on the basis of your perception, memory, communication, and appearance. Your overall image as a witness will count a great deal in persuading the arbitrator or hearing officer to accept, as fact, your testimony.

Appearance and Image

1. Wear neat clean clothes. Conservative attire is the best. In most cases the type of clothing you normally wear to work will be appropriate, even if it is a uniform.
2. Don't smoke or chew gum while testifying or while in the hearing room.
3. You should sit upright. Don't slump down into the chair.
4. Don't fidget in your chair or with your pens, rings, papers, or other objects. Don't grip the arms of the chair or table. Leave your hands free.
5. Show a respectful attitude to all those present at the hearing, even though your true feelings may be different. This includes contact with others outside the hearing room during breaks and recesses.

Answering Questions

6. Tell the truth. Just answer the question to the best of your ability and memory. Don't exaggerate.
7. Listen carefully to the questions. Don't formulate an answer until the question has been fully stated. Do not answer a question unless you completely understand it. If you don't understand the question, ask for clarification.

8. Pause and think before answering any question. Take your time before answering any question and do not permit yourself to be hurried.
9. Do not attempt to memorize your testimony.
10. Only answer the question. As a general rule, avoid volunteering information. In some cases a question can't be truthfully answered with a "yes" or "no." You then have a right to explain the answer.
11. If your answer is wrong, correct it immediately.
12. If your answer is unclear, clarify it immediately.
13. Always speak distinctly and in a strong voice that can be clearly heard. Don't nod your head for a "yes" or "no" answer.
14. Don't cover your mouth with your hand while speaking.
15. Maintain good eye contact with the arbitrator or hearing officer or with the questioner. Don't look around the room, at the table, or at the ceiling while answering questions.
16. If an objection has been made to a question, stop testifying immediately. Proceed with your response only when you have been told to answer the question. You may want the question repeated.
17. Don't lose your temper or argue. On cross-examination, advocates frequently try to get witnesses to lose their temper. Don't fall for this trick. Just answer the questions truthfully.
18. If asked about details you can't remember, say you don't remember. It is not necessary for you to remember every detail.
19. If your response to a question is an estimate, be sure to say it is only an estimate. This most often happens when there are questions about time, dates, distances, and speeds.
20. When you are testifying you are on your own. The employer's advocate can't help you answer the questions. If

If the question is improper, the employer's advocate will make an objection.

21. Answer questions with plain, simple words. Avoid use of slang or technical words. If such words must be used, explain the meaning of the terms. The arbitrator or hearing officer must be able to understand what you are saying.
22. Be well prepared on the subject on which you will be testifying. Review your records and notes before coming to the hearing, but don't memorize your answers. It is permissible for you to refer to your own notes and records while testifying. These should be well organized so you can refer to items quickly. The opposing counsel has the right to inspect any notes or records you refer to during your testimony. If there is something you don't want others to see, don't bring it to the hearing.
23. If you are asked whether you have talked to anybody about the case, tell the truth. Arbitrators and hearing officers know that good advocates always talk to the witnesses before they testify.

Outside the hearing

24. Be careful not to discuss the case with others. Don't discuss the case in halls, rest rooms, or elsewhere in the building, except with the employer's advocate.
25. Don't discuss the case in restaurants, stores, or other places where you can be overheard. You never know who might overhear the conversation.